The Captain's Year

The Captain's Year

*A first-hand account of a season
in the life of a professional
cricketer and captain*

Alan Wells

TWO HEADS
PUBLISHING

First published in 1994 by

Two Heads Publishing
12A Franklyn Suite
The Priory
Haywards Heath
West Sussex
RH16 3LB

ISBN   1-897850-60-3

Photograph credits
South Africa - Wayne Morton.
All others by Roger Ockenden.

Printed by Caldra House Ltd., Hove, Sussex
Bound by Marba Bookbinders, London

For Melanie and Luke
and my parents

THE PRINCIPLE CHARACTERS

Norman Gifford MBE - The Sussex Cricket Manager. Giffy allows me to benefit from his experience by encouraging me to follow my instincts. A major influence on my development as a captain.

Bill Athey - Billy's even temperament and experience brings the vital quality of stability to the side. He is the first to allocate nicknames.

Neil Lenham - known as *Pin* because he has the smallest head in the world. He is the oldest twenty-eight year old on the circuit and seems to have been in the side longer than anyone else.

Jamie Hall - The comedian of the side and also a record-breaker. After taking 304 minutes to score fifty at The Oval he is known as *JK*, after John Lever. He has never before left so many balls outside the off-stump.

David Smith - Smithy, the smartest dresser on the circuit, has been instrumental in my development as a batsman. Despite his reputation as a tough guy, he bears the brunt of dressing room jokes.

Martin Speight - Speighty is a consummate artist, with bat and brush. One of the most naturally gifted batsmen playing cricket today.

Peter Moores - *Action Man* is a fitness fanatic and one of the top keepers on the circuit. A confidant and guiding light on and off the field.

Keith Greenfield - Has the largest family in Brighton, including an uncle who telephoned a Radio 5 sports programme to ask how someone who had scored a century against Sierra Leone *sic* could possibly be left out of the first-team. As Sussex as Brighton Rock.

Carlos Remy - Now showing signs of realising his potential as a gifted all-rounder. A valuable contributor to both our one-day and championship cricket.

Franklyn Stephenson - *Cookie* has this year earned a new nickname - *The Busker* - after his antics on the London Underground. Guitar-strumming, fun-loving with staggering self-belief. An inspiration with the ball and often returns to the pavilion wondering not why he played a rash shot but how he missed the ball!

Paul Jarvis - Jarv's experience is an invaluable asset. He has released Ed Giddins from the pressure of the new ball and is a perfect partner for Franklyn. A captain's dream, he is a dedicated cricketer and one of the fittest men in the side.

Ian Salisbury - Sals is a bowler of undisputed class as well as a useful bat and a fine close-fielder. He is also a practical joker who shows no mercy to his team-mates.

Eddie Hemmings - The most experienced man on the circuit and a real club man. He took his 1500th wicket this summer and likes nothing more than to pass the time with Sussex members.

Jason Lewry - Christened *Urcho* by Billy Athey, after a character in 'Planet of the Apes.' Cool, calm and confident.

Ed Giddins - Giddo is a fast bowler of enormous promise who has come of age this year and was rewarded with his county cap. Last winter he worked as a topless waiter in Australia and is not averse to a touch of modelling - he's not known as the *Diamond Geezer* for nothing.

FOREWORD

Last summer, for the first time for as long as he would care to remember, Alan Wells had a rotten time with the bat. Odd really, since he has become one of the game's outstanding players, fit to sit alongside the Gooches and Gattings, Smiths and Hicks that rule the roost in county cricket. He is a brave and prolific run-scorer, capable of winning matches with his intelligent, underrated strokeplay.

It is ironic then that he chose to chronicle his life in a year when his form deserted him. It makes for a good read however, since the warts-and-all nature of personal disappointment is far more revealing than a tale covered in glory. When Simon Barnes, in his book *"Horse, Sweat and Tears"* followed a racing season from inside the stables of John Dunlop, the most revealing chapters came at a time when the stable was in depression after a catalogue of misfortunes had denied them any winners.

In no way, of course, have Sussex suffered misfortune, in fact they threatened to win the county championship until the awesome Warwickshire juggernaut came to Hove in late August. Wells saw a side of leadership that he will not have known and it will stand him in the best possible stead for the tour of India that awaits him as captain of the England A team.

Of all the positions of power on the playing side in modern sport, few ask more of a man than to lead his county cricket team. Unlike the football manager, who also sets the standard for the approach, performance and results of his team, the cricket captain cannot stand back with objectivity; cannot castigate without self-examination; cannot instruct and advise, cajole and encourage, hire and fire without recourse to his own performance. In short he is an active part of the team and must be able to practise in the way that he preaches.

This can be awkward, since form is an unreliable, elusive thing that deserts you suddenly and leaves you vulnerable to criticism. Graham Gooch, who stood down after his first season as captain of Essex said ruefully, *"When you win you are supposed to and when you lose it is your fault."* Though he was back in the job two years later, and then carried the responsibility both for Essex and England, better than most in this frenetic modern age, the burden weighed heavily on his rolling shoulders and had, at first, affected even his quite exceptional batting. The real gift of good captaincy is an ability to pull the strings even when personally exposed.

Prior to Alan, Sussex had such a man in John Barclay, the lively Etonian who took his county so close to the Championship in 1981. Garth le Roux thought Barclay to be the best captain he played under and rated him an all-rounder who, if struggling for form with bat or ball, still made the most essential contribution as captain. Barclay thought the job to be more demanding than any executive role in commerce or industry, let alone running a football team!

Alan has had to respond to those great traditions in Sussex cricket. Less than nine months ago he was with England A, pioneering in South Africa, and played somewhere near his best. Last summer he led Sussex with his usual unbridled enthusiasm and absolute toughness - he is not one to suffer mediocrity or immaturity - and briefly it seemed they might prevail. Though it was not to be, he has an exciting, demanding winter ahead, for India holds many secrets and much fascination. The tour will be a good test for a popular figure and a fine batsman and I am certain he will enjoy leading his young England team more than he can imagine.

They are lucky to have him, and we are lucky to have his diary. *The Captain's Year* gives a telling insight and should inform lovers of the game at all levels of the blood, sweat and tears that make cricket so compelling.

Mark Nicholas
October 1994

INTRODUCTION

A year in the life of a professional cricketer is never uneventful. I started the year on tour to South Africa with England A and finish this season looking forward to captaining England A on the winter tour to India. The year has turned full circle.

At Sussex I have the challenge of leading what I believe to be the most talented and balanced side on the circuit. Not all of our potential has been realised this year, but it has been an exciting summer when Sussex remained in contention for the Championship right up until the last few games. It takes time and progressive management to blend talent and experience into a winning combination and our major achievement of this year is to have laid the foundations for success in the years ahead.

Players such as Jamie Hall and Neil Lenham are maturing into accomplished batsmen who command a regular place in the side. Paul Jarvis has added pace and experience to the bowling attack, and with youngsters such as Jason Lewry getting his first taste of county cricket, there is more to come. The under-rated Ed Giddins took fifty wickets for the first time in his career, was awarded his county cap, and is a bowler to watch for the future. Franklyn Stephenson thrilled us all with inspirational performances with bat and ball. Billy Athey and David Smith provided stability and experience. Peter Moores was at my side for the whole summer offering help and advice. Eddie Hemmings turned in a vintage performance and Ian Salisbury demonstrated that he is a Test bowler. Martin Speight continued to amaze us all with his exuberant batting.

Every player makes a contribution as an individual but it is the captain's task to pull it all together, on and off the field. To navigate the whole team through the trials and tribulations of a cricket season. To travel the length and breadth of the country and to occasionally spend time at home with his family. To cajole, motivate and sometimes discipline his team-mates, both old sweats and young pros. To cope with the highs of winning and the lows of losing. To maintain his own form as a player as well as cultivating the skills of others. In my view there is no better job in the world and there is nothing else I'd rather be doing.

Readers of this book, and Sussex members in particular, might wonder if it has had any influence on my performances in a season during which I failed to score the runs people expected of me. There is but one aim I set out to achieve with this book: to provide an insight into a year in the life of a professional cricketer and captain. It is also a unique record of Sussex's 1994 season. I can assure readers that nothing interferes with my desire for Alan Wells to score runs and Sussex to win games.

29 November 1993 - England A in South Africa

My wife Melanie, with my little son Luke, dropped me off at the airport to start my first official tour to South Africa. A pretty emotional moment really. I am already looking forward to seeing them again at Christmas.

I recall the ill-fated Gatting tour, and my ban from representing England, but it is with a keen sense of anticipation that I approach this tour. I was never subject to any open hostility from other players when I toured South Africa in an unofficial capacity, but I remember barbed words in print from Derek Pringle and Angus Fraser, especially when the five-year ban was reduced to three. On the domestic circuit animosity never materialised on the pitch. At the time, the thought of offering a defence never entered my mind. It was a matter of realising an ambition to play cricket at the highest level. In any case, the situation was extremely volatile and opposing views had polarised. The advice at the time from David Graveney and Ali Bacher was to avoid being drawn into a debate which would only be seen as a futile justification. I spent several years coaching promising black youngsters at Langa township, a place we will be visiting and playing at on this tour. County pros were never given any credit for helping SACU execute and develop their now much praised coaching schemes. I was aware that facilities were not what they should be but I felt that a positive contribution was being made, plus I was plying my trade. It was at times a hair-raising experience but one that I thoroughly enjoyed, and I am looking forward to being in Langa again.

On the flight to Johannesburg we drank some champagne, toasted each other's health and good luck on the tour, hoping that it will be a champagne trip on the field as well as off. The in-flight entertainment brings me quickly down to earth. The sports channel on the inward flight to London features last season's Nat West final between Sussex and Warwickshire. I do not want to live through that nightmare again. The programme guide has a picture of me being bowled around my legs by the off-spinner.

We left England full of confidence. The guys are all in good nick and are looking forward to a successful tour. Everybody is very confident and anxious to prove themselves worthy of greater things, as well as looking forward to performing well as a team. I will be going flat out to score as many runs as I possibly can with the forthcoming tour to the West Indies in the back of my mind. A personal target for next summer is to prove that I could contribute at Test level. I still feel disappointment at not being selected for the main tour but as one of the senior players on this tour, it is up to me to perform.

30 November

Preparing for a press conference with captain Hugh Morris and the team managers, Phil Neale and Bob Bennett. No doubt I'll be questioned on comparisons between this tour and the infamous Gatting tour three years ago. In the end it was far more relaxed than the last press conference I endured on the 'rebel' tour. Ali Bacher was present and it is good to see his happy face again. He has worked wonders to put South African cricket back on the map and he looks proud to welcome the first official England touring party to visit South Africa for twenty-nine years. He has fought hard to rebuild South African cricket and it is fitting that the first match will be in Alexandra Township, against a Transvaal Invitation XI. After the press conference a few journalists asked me about the tour and how I felt about returning to South Africa. It was all very positive and I was pleased to inform them that I was happy to be back.

There has been a lot of talk about the dress code. We are all given sheets of paper with the dress code laid out so we know exactly what to wear, where and when. It is both amusing and confusing because for the first four days of the trip we have to wear Whittingdale clothing because, as we haven't yet started a game, we are effectively still training. When we start playing we switch to Tetley, the official sponsors. After the debate over the sartorial standards set in India, the dress code is a sensitive issue, so Bob Bennett has rightly made it clear that we will be properly dressed at all times - nets included. Once we were in the right clothes, we went to the ground and did our first bit of fielding practice.

1 December

Nets all day. The wickets are a bit uneven and more enjoyable for the bowlers than for the batsmen. Afterwards we congregated in the players' room with refreshments courtesy of the sponsors. The team is coming together very well and it is going to be a general rule that when we get back from the ground all the players will get together over a beer or two before they all go their separate ways in the evening. During this gathering Bob Bennett put on a video tape entitled 'Great One-Day Finishes', and many of them go back into the late 'seventies and early 'eighties. This was an interesting experience for me as I suddenly realised that I am one of the senior players on the tour. Few of us here have played against some of the players featured in the video - Barry Wood, Andy Roberts, Joel Garner, Ian Botham et al. To the younger players this makes me an old hand! It's good to think that some of the players will see me as an experienced batsman and, as the tour progresses, providing I score some runs, I might be able to assist them with their own game. I have already had a chat with John Crawley about one or two things and it gives me a lot of pleasure that the guys actually do respect that I have been around a few years, and they can talk to me about the technical side of things and how to approach the game.

I am only 32 and should have seven or eight playing years at least left in the game and hopefully, one day, I'll play at the highest level. Even now I find myself thinking ahead about coaching or managing. I believe that I have a lot to offer as far as batting is concerned, not only on the technical side but also on the psychological aspects which are so important in cricket. In common with many players, I have gone through bad times and good times, and I think that really has helped me cope with the highs and lows which come with playing professional cricket. It gives you real strength of character and I think that it is the sort of experience that would be valuable to emerging players. They will obviously have the same experiences, and if there is someone around to help them, somebody who has been there before and come through it, as I have, then it will obviously give them a great deal of confidence. It is something that I never had as a young player at Sussex. People were not very forthcoming with advice and help, and that is something that I have always regretted. I feel that if somebody had helped me discover myself and my game then I might have had an opportunity to tour before the tender age of 32, with what is basically an England second team.

It was only when David Smith joined us from Surrey and Norman Gifford came along as Cricket Manager, that I really felt a more complete player. I was a developed player and a senior batsman at the club but there were still elements of the jigsaw missing, and those two guys really put the pieces together for me. I sometimes think what might have been if that had happened ten years earlier.

Since becoming captain of Sussex, I have realised how important communication, leadership and management is to the game of cricket. At some stage later in my career I could see myself remaining in the game in a role where my experience can be put to good use. Good communication is essential. It is all well and good identifying flaws in technique but how these are rectified is another matter, not just dependent on technical skill. The more experiences you have lived through, the better you can communicate with a player.

You can empathise with them when things are going wrong, and share the good times when things are going right.

2 December

Went to the British Consulate, along with 300 other people, for a buffet supper hosted by the Ambassador. A couple of speeches were made about how important it was for the England side to be back in the country, which made us feel good. Talking to people at the Consulate, particularly the South Africans, it became clear that they did not really know us and it made me feel for the first time that we really are an England second team. This really frustrated me and made me even more determined not to be labelled as second-string. We met one guy who annoyed me because he was from Bognor Regis originally, and although he moved to South Africa when he was very young, he has since given up all allegiance to England, which I could not understand. In a patronising way he ridiculed the MCC tie we were wearing, saying it looked like something from Marks & Spencer! Needless to say he did not understand cricket too well, but even so it was pretty insulting.

In many ways tonight reminded me of my first trip to South Africa as a 19 year old back in 1981, having completed my first year on the staff with Sussex. I went to Queenstown and coached at Queens College for a season. One of the many talented youngsters I coached there was Daryll Cullinan, then a raw teenager but clearly a player with a great future ahead of him. It gave me a thrill to see him walk to the crease to bat for South Africa against Australia in a Test match.

When I was coaching at Queens I remember going into a bar and some South Africans were really getting stuck into me because although I was a professional cricketer nobody had heard of me. *"You are just a young Englishman . . . you are nothing . . ."* and so on. This verbal attack, combined with feeling homesick at the time, upset me to the extent that it actually reduced me to tears. Even so, it was one of those incidents that just made me even more determined to succeed as a cricketer.

3 December

Today was spent practising at the Wanderers ground, including an excellent session in the middle. Prior to practice we were briefed on tomorrow's game at Alexandra Township. Three years ago the people of Alex set out to watch the Gatting side play South Africa, but every time they approached the Wanderers stadium they were stopped by policemen carrying tear-gas, truncheons and guns. When England A open the tour at the Alexandra Oval, built on an old rubbish dump, it will be big day in South African sport because it is the first time any touring side has played in this township. The political significance far outweighs the importance of the cricket, and this is amply demonstrated by the lack of facilities and the unevenness of the Astroturf wicket. It will be the sort of match where the occasion means more than the result.

It is very important that we win this game because the press are out here and, as ever, they are looking for any early hiccup. So I think it is vital that we approach the game with the right attitude and it is right of the management to forewarn us of the elements outside of our control, and encourage the team to actually go out there, play cricket, and win the game for England. We will be playing against some quality players as well as talented youngsters out to impress, so we have got to really concentrate on our jobs and win what could be a difficult game.

4 December - Transvaal Invitation XI at Alexandra

The journey from the hotel to the ground may have taken only ten minutes but it took us into another world for the first game of the tour, against a Transvaal Invitation XI. It was an amazing experience because the ground overlooks the shanty-town of the township. I have been into townships to coach before, but never actually played a game of cricket in one. It was really quite an experience for the guys to witness how black people are expected to live out here. However many times I come back to South Africa, I can never get to grips with the fact that you can travel past houses worth literally millions of Rand, with swimming pools, tennis courts, security guards and acres of land. Then turn a corner and witness the poverty of Alexandra Township. There are some visible signs of improvement but things have to change sooner rather than later. Not surprisingly, it was very quiet on the coach and even the players who have been to Pakistan and India were moved by the view from the windows. It was not surprising that at the ground the locals were outnumbered by VIP's and media.

As far as the cricket was concerned, the artificial wicket was atrocious, despite having been imported from home and paid for by the Bank of England! It was a Nottinghamshire wicket: uneven and dangerously bouncy at times. The outfield was incredibly slow. Some of the shots I played were hit like tracer bullets and still did not reach the boundary. The fielder did not even have to run around from third man to cut the ball off. It felt like trying to hit the ball through water or sand. Believe it or not we managed to scrape 121 in just short of 44 overs. Mal Loye played really well and top-scored with 38. I made 29, and the only other double figure contribution was from Steve Rhodes. The bowlers did well: Dominic Cork took six for nine in less than eight overs. We beat them by 43 runs and it has done us good to get a win under our belt at this early stage.

It was a very awkward pitch to bat on, but I am a great believer in trying to take something positive from a difficult situation. I scratched around like an old hen out there for an hour or so, hitting only one boundary, but I came away feeling as though I had achieved something, because I came through a really dodgy early spell and battled my way through for the side.

Naturally, public relations were more important than the cricket. Nobody complained about the facilities - how could we, when the local people have to endure the squalor only one good hit away over mid-wicket.

Bob Bennett presented community leaders with Kwik cricket sets donated by the TCCB and both Hugh Morris and Phil Neale were very pleased with the professional way the team approached all aspects of the game. Mandy Yachad, the international opener, and the Test player Mark Rushmere played against us along with Clive Eksteen, a left-arm spinner. The teenage Sowetan captain Geoffrey Toyana won the Man of the Match award. Although it was a fun day, the cricket was still very competitive. The South Africans really wanted to beat us, there is no doubt about that.

Batting here was a strange experience for me in more ways than one. When I finally nicked a ball down to third man I thought to myself, "Well that's my first run for an official England side." It made me feel really proud.

6 December - Western Transvaal at Potchefstroom

Up at 5.30am to travel to Potchefstroom to play against Western Transvaal. We lost the toss and they put us in. We ended up getting 260 for six. Hugh Morris batted well, John Crawley scored a talented 88, and I managed 61. I felt really good and it was productive to spend some time in the middle with Transvaal coming up at the end of the week. The opposition finished with 178 for seven and at 82 runs short were never really in the game. Martin McCague bowled well and all the batsmen, with the exception of Mark Lathwell, have shown decent form. Mark doesn't appear to let things worry him, but he is introspective and it's difficult to fathom what he is thinking.

In the field today I was thinking about my role as vice-captain compared with the job of captaining the side. As captain you are concentrating on every ball, every field placing, bowling changes and the like. As a fielder you are thinking of saving the single, taking a catch, but when you are captain the level of concentration required is altogether on another level.

Fortunately, touring is not all about early starts. The other day I played golf with Mal Loye, Robert Croft and Peter Such and it made me appreciate just how lucky I am to be able to earn a living playing cricket. Not that there aren't young players who moan about their lot in the professional game. The evening after the game we had a discussion about the differences in salary structures at the various counties. I think a few of the guys were surprised when I actually told them that the first time I ever asked for more money was after my second year of captaincy at Sussex - 12 or 13 years of professional cricket without asking for a rise! A few of the younger guys, especially those who have been involved in Test matches, were shocked. Not that money isn't important, but doing well for Sussex and myself has always come first. After five good years on the trot, two years as captain, and reaching the Nat West final, I felt that I was worth a few quid more than what was offered.

7 December

Our first full day off and we enjoyed a fantastic day at Sun City. The million-dollar golf classic had just finished and we had the pleasure of meeting Nick Faldo pool-side at the Palace hotel. Wayne Morton the physio, Martin McCague, Mark Ilott and myself were photographed with Faldo wearing the England physio's cap - one for the benefit brochure. The surroundings and facilities are stunning: it's just not what you expect to find in the middle of the bush.

Melanie would love a holiday here. Every night I look at the photographs of Melanie and my son Luke, and it makes me feel like calling home all the time. I do call occasionally, but the lot of a touring cricketer, however enjoyable and privileged, doesn't allow for luxuries such as daily calls home from South Africa. I admire the way the Robin Smiths and Graham Goochs of this world spend twelve months a year playing cricket, away from their young families. It is obviously something you get used to, but with the level of concentration needed to play professional cricket, it can't be easy.

8 December - Eastern Transvaal at Springs

Another one-day game, against Eastern Transvaal, in the Afrikaans town of Springs. Another emphatic win. Mark Lathwell hit 133 and yours truly made 37 not out. Although some of us are in competition with each other, in case a replacement is needed for the West Indies tour, it does not detract from an excellent team spirit and mutual support amongst the players. We are after all representing England and we all feel that our individual cause will be advanced if we return as a successful team.

After the game we went to see Northern Transvaal

comprehensively thrash Natal, captained by Malcolm Marshall. Although we have three one-day wins under our belt, the first real test against quality opposition will be the four-day game with Transvaal coming up. A feature of the Northern Transvaal versus Natal game was hundreds of young kids all over the field with bats and balls, gloves and pads. It was a thrill to see so many youngsters completely enthralled with cricket, playing with a straight bat and with good bowling actions too! This is just one province in South Africa and it makes you wonder how strong the national side will be in ten years.

Sitting in front of the TV watching South Africa beating Australia reminds me what tough opposition England will face next summer. For a team back in world cricket for such a short space of time they have made impressive progress.

10 December - Transvaal at Wanderers, first day

Our opening first-class tour match. A grassy wicket, they decided to bat and we bowled them out for 161. A fine effort against a side with players the calibre of Jimmy Cook, Mark Rushmere and Mike Haysman. We lost Hugh Morris early on, but Lathwell and Crawley put on over 100 until Crawley was unluckily run-out for 44. I was out for seven with only a few overs to go to a ball which kept low and nipped back. Lathwell progressed smoothly and seemed to be more secure, exercising discretion in playing balls outside off-stump.

It is interesting to observe how the guys react to success and failure in our first big game. Mark Ilott has bowled well in every respect and although we have won every game, he is disappointed at not taking more wickets. Team success and individual success doesn't always go hand-in-hand. As a professional sportsman you have to stay on an even keel: enjoy the high of a good individual performance but remember the importance of achieving as a team. Last season I felt the pressure of my own good performances when I was talked about as a possible for the West Indies tour. I have a favourite saying hanging on my wall, *"Grant me the serenity to accept the things I cannot change, the power to change the things I can, and the wisdom to know the difference."* This is a reliable metaphor for life as well as cricket and when I'm feeling down thinking of this really helps me. I'll pin it to the inside of my cricket coffin!

11 December - Transvaal, second day

We reached almost 300, giving us a healthy lead. We took two early wickets and the day ended with Transvaal still 32 behind. With the likes of Jimmy Cook coming in at five, we'll have to work hard to dismiss them and give ourselves an easy run-chase to win the game.

I'm concerned about my failure in the first innings. I don't normally dwell on these things but this has been bothering me. I need to keep my name in the frame and cannot afford to fail on this tour. As a result I feel I'm putting myself under undue pressure. This tour is a real chance to prove myself and to feel as nervous as I did walking out to bat in the first innings is uncharacteristic and indicative of what could be at stake. It's a battle to stop myself forcing runs and I need to relax and approach my batting in a less anxious state of mind. My game is up to it and so is my mind, so it's up to me and I know I'll do it.

12 December - Transvaal, third day
One of the most extraordinary and memorable days first-class cricket I have ever participated in. Only three of us around at breakfast and I said to Peter Such *"Where is everyone else?"* The physio came in and announced that six of the guys had gone down overnight with a virus. My first reaction was to think of how we could take the field with only two bowlers - Peter Such and Mark Ilott - with me and Mark Lathwell as fill-ins. Wayne Morton, in true Yorkshire fashion, somehow got everyone on the coach and to the ground. The umpires and Jimmy Cook kindly agreed to a delayed start although I remained sceptical that the team could take the field. The bulldog spirit won through and Gough and Cork made a partial recovery. The other four, including the captain, returned to the hotel. The Wanderers' new all-singing-and-dancing electronic scoreboard announced a delay due to illness.

We started at 1pm and Mark Ilott performed heroics, bowling for a complete session and taking six wickets. Standing at slip it occurred to me that, with Hugh Morris back in the hotel, I was captaining an England side - a fantastic thrill. The physio was on as a substitute fielder, as were the coach Phil Neale, the 12th, 13th, and 14th man! Given our depleted team, it was a fantastic effort to bowl them out for 200. Removing Jimmy Cook for only nine was very pleasing. I set a bat-pad on the leg side, and another at wide mid-on, and we obviously had a fine leg. Cook doesn't really get out of his crease and tends to come half forward to a ball swinging in, just pushing it through mid-wicket. Mark Ilott was swinging the ball in and after consulting with Steve Rhodes, I moved Mark Lathwell deeper and straighter at bat-pad to force Cook to play square and perhaps across the ball. A few balls later, Cook played across one and was lbw. It is pleasing as a captain when a minor adjustment or tactic pays off.

There was a unique atmosphere and the crowd responded to our fighting spirit. Darren Gough had to go off after a five over spell, we had a catch off a no-ball, a missed run-out and Rushmere was dropped. Everything was happening. What we at first thought would be a farce turned into a thrilling game of cricket. There was no mickey-taking of the coach and physio on the field; the jokes were left behind in the dressing room. At tea they were eight down with a lead of 60-odd and there was no shortage of advice on what to do to remove the last two on resumption of play. My initial thought was to bowl Peter Such and this was vindicated with his first ball to Jack after tea. It span, bounced, inside edge onto the pad, looped towards a nonexistent square-leg, and Steve Rhodes ran round to take a superb diving catch. Two balls later, Such removed the number 11 and they were all out, leaving us 69 to win.

Rhodes and Lathwell opened the innings. Jack

bounced Lathwell first ball and he hooked it straight down the throat of fine leg. Lathwell has a terrific temperament; a fine 83 in the first innings and a first-baller in the second, but not a flicker of emotion at either. A real contrast to Mark Ilott. With Crawley and Morris sick, I was batting at three. We knocked off the remaining runs in the last session. Despite the fact that I didn't bat too well, and was dropped early on, I managed to hit the winning runs and we won by nine wickets with a day to spare.

A. C. Smith, the TCCB Chief Executive, witnessed the game and was delighted that we won under such adverse circumstances. A few of the boys were low on cash, with a couple of days to go before the next expenses hand-out, and A. C. Smith came to the rescue on behalf of the TCCB to pay for golf the next day; a nice gesture.

15 December - Eastern Province Invitation XI at Zwide
Our second township goodwill match today, at Zwide, just outside Port Elizabeth, and we completed our fifth successive tour win with some ease. We scored 189 on a very slow wicket and they failed to reach 100 in reply. The game was a real community event and was attended by Ali Bacher along with other leading members of the cricket union and Eastern Province Cricket Development Unit. The lunchtime speeches and talk amongst the local youngsters was about more than cricket. They spoke of the major social changes to come and there was a tangible feeling that a brighter and more equal South Africa is just around the corner. The

happy and smiling youngsters around us should be the first generation to benefit from the new South Africa. A post-match tour of the township soon put things into perspective.

16 December

At breakfast Bob Bennett produced cuttings from the English press regarding the drama of the Transvaal game. Two reports particularly, with headlines such as *'Management Under Fire'*, were very negative and implied that the tour management virtually forced sick players to take the field, against doctor's orders. This slating approach is so hard to understand after such a great team performance. The tour so far has been very successful and completely harmonious, and I suppose it is inevitable that the press will look for negative aspects to fill out their copy, but it is a sad distortion of the facts behind a happy and contented tour.

Port Elizabeth is quite a contrast to Jo'burg and our hotel facilities here leave something to be desired. During a short meeting it became apparent that some of the guys were on a downer after leaving behind the great facilities in Jo'burg. Bob Bennett was quick to organise a team meal, on the TCCB, at a superb local restaurant. We had a terrific night out and it was a real tonic for all the players. It didn't seem to make the press back home though.

17 December - Eastern Province at St. George's Park, first day

The first day of a four-day game against Eastern

Province, captained by Eldine Baptiste, who inexplicably put us in to bat after winning the toss. We played well on a good wicket and reached 310 for two after Lathwell got out early on to what he admitted was a poor shot. John Crawley is 150 not out after a brilliant knock and I batted with him for much of the last session, to finish on 51. At a mere 23 years of age, Crawley has a very mature approach to cricket and life, and I feel sure he will go on to play for England at Test level.

After the drama of sickness in Jo'burg we had a 50-minute stoppage in play when the electrically-operated sightscreen stuck on an advertisement for Opel cars due to a power cut. The umpire managed to fix the screen and play resumed.

18 December - Eastern Province, second day

Another great day for batting. John Crawley and I enjoyed a partnership of 250 with Crawley finishing on a magnificent career best 286, without giving a chance apart from a sticky period in the 160s when I helped him through by playing my shots at the other end. I made 126, my thirty-third first-class century, and the sort of aggressive innings when I was able to demonstrate how I can play. Although I have achieved a lot in the last few years, I still feel the need to prove myself, although the facts speak for themselves and I know that self-doubt shouldn't be part of my game. I felt very relaxed and played the sort of shots I don't think twice about at home. When I was out there batting, my first thought of making a century didn't come until I was in the nineties and it was late in the evening before it sank in that although I'd spent yet another day in the office, I had scored my first hundred for an England side. What made it more special was that Melanie and Luke arrived in Cape Town today and I'm looking forward to seeing them for the first time in three weeks. We declared on 566 for five and they finished the day on 127 for eight, after great bowling spells from Robert Croft and Dominic Cork. The atmosphere in the field was terrific and the team is reaping the dividend from the right balance of youth and experience.

19 December - Eastern Province, third day
We wrapped up the Eastern Province first innings when Robert Croft acted successfully on a suggestion of mine to slightly adjust his line against their obdurate number nine. He playfully told me how useful it was to have *". . an old bugger who has been around a while"* in the side to help out youngsters such as himself. It's indicative of the spirit in the team that advice is freely given and accepted between the experienced and less experienced players. They are young and ambitious and I'm not sure whether they realise that players such as me are also fighting for recognition and are as hungry as anyone to be considered for the senior England side.

Making inroads into their second innings was harder going and they dug in to finish the day on 185 for four. It was the first day on the whole tour when everything hadn't gone our way, but the young players responded well.

20 December - Eastern Province, final day

Eldine Baptiste was out to his first ball of the day and after that it was a matter of bowling well, staying patient and taking the remaining wickets. It was a good win by an innings and 70 runs and there were jubilant scenes in the dressing room afterwards. During this game there was a bit of sledging, both from our bowlers, and from one of their bowlers aimed at me, to which I responded in no uncertain terms. Hugh Morris held a team meeting and made it clear that sledging of any kind isn't acceptable. I had to apologise to Hugh for an over zealous appeal for a caught behind off Martin McCague's bowling. Bob Bennett later berated the seam bowlers for not limiting their aggression to bowling, and said there was no need to offer abuse and swearing to fire themselves up. A fair comment really, given the propensity of the press to focus on events of this kind. The TCCB are generally very sensitive about sledging and it always comes up at captains' meetings at home, and rightly so, as they are paranoid about it permeating through to county level. It was ironic to see a press cutting from *The Sun* showing a glaring Martin McCague in his follow-through with an equally glaring headline of *"Martin McGob."* Thankfully it is something that rarely surfaces in county games.

Last year's captains' meeting at Lords was more interesting than most. In the wake of the Pakistan tour, the debate about ball-tampering was still raging, and we were informed that at the end of every over the ball would go to the square-leg umpire for inspection.

Naturally, someone asked how the umpires would know whether the ball had been interfered with. We were told that as the TCCB have the ball from the controversial England versus Pakistan Test, the umpires would know exactly what to look for!

22 December

This morning Phil Neale insisted on an early fielding practice session, for one hour. All a bit superfluous after two days in the field at Port Elizabeth. A full day of rest would not have gone amiss, with an early start tomorrow for the game at Langa township, and a net session to follow on Christmas Eve, not to mention my self-inflicted sunburn!

23 December - Western Province Invitation XI at Langa

A steaming hot day at Langa township and I had the honour of captaining an England side for the first time in my career. I coached at Langa several years ago and was delighted to be playing against Ben Malamba, one of my most promising pupils from that time. The nets hadn't changed but the ground now sports a grass wicket instead of an artificial strip. I won the toss and decided to bat on a poor wicket with a 'hill' just back off a length which made the ball balloon up like a tennis ball. We altered the order to accommodate the guys in need of batting practice, and when I came out to bat we were 19 for four, after only five overs. I made 65 out of a total of 170 in 45 overs. They reached 151 and proved to be stronger opposition than we expected, but it was a pleasing performance and our seventh win on the trot. I batted with the self-belief that is needed to generate a good performance under pressure, as we were in real danger failing to score enough runs to win the match.

I need to feel an inner-arrogance and self-belief in my batting. It reminded me of an occasion a few years ago when we played Warwickshire at Eastbourne. On the Saturday in the championship match I was out first ball and same again in the Sunday League game. Over dinner with David Smith the talk naturally turned to cricket and my batting in particular. Smithy told me that as far as I had come in the game there was still something lacking in my batting, a self-belief that I was the best player on the field. It may have been coincidence that in my next innings I scored 140 not out, but from that day on I took his advice to heart. You don't have to strut or show arrogance outwardly, but you must believe inside that the opposition feels that they must get you out or you are going to accumulate runs against them. He told me that as far as he was concerned, this was the last and probably the most difficult hurdle to overcome if I was to become a complete batsman. Up until the Port Elizabeth game, the feeling of needing to prove myself to those around me was stifling my self-belief, but it is back with me now.

25 December
Christmas with my family by the swimming pool in the sun and my little boy is finding it hard to get used to the idea that it is actually Christmas. In the evening we

enjoyed a team meal, again courtesy of the TCCB, with wives and girlfriends, but we were mindful of our game coming up tomorrow.

26 December - Western Province at Newlands, first day

First day of a four-day game against Western Province. The bowlers kept to a disciplined line and length and made runs hard to get. They were all out for 177 and we finished the day on 74 for two. Western Province is one of the stronger sides and we'll need to bat well tomorrow for a first innings lead, and then bowl well to win the match.

27 December - Western Province, second day

I was 12 not out overnight and managed to double my score before being given out caught behind from a ball which hit my pad. A bit frustrating, but an easy mistake to make as the ball did sound as if it hit the edge. Apart from a feeling of disappointment, I felt in good form and I accept these things as part and parcel of the game. Mal Loye rode his luck to get 68 and help us to a total of 321. Mal is a young player and sometimes prone to impetuosity in his choice of shot, but he'll overcome this with experience.

28 December - Western Province, third day

With Darren Gough taking four wickets, Mark Ilott three, Dominic Cork two and Robert Croft one, we bowled them out for 178. Again, we performed well as a team and a feature of our cricket so far has been the constant pressure we apply when bowling. There have been few occasions when an opposing batsman has got on top of one of our bowlers, and when it has happened we have been able to tie-up one end and keep the brakes on. Hugh Morris and Mark Lathwell knocked off the 35 runs required for us to record our eighth successive win. Standing at slip, alongside Hugh Morris and Steve Rhodes, we reflected on the realisation that this has been the most successful run of victories we have been involved in. The guys have earned a day off tomorrow and will no doubt spend most of it on the beach. For Melanie and myself it is a special day as it is Luke's third birthday.

30 December
Up early and spent a couple of hours with my family before a tearful goodbye with me heading off to Durban. It is always sad to say goodbye but doubly so on this occasion as they will be staying in Cape Town until the 12th of January and I'll be elsewhere in the country. The other wives have travelled to Durban and it was sorely tempting to bring Melanie and Luke with me. Spending time with my family has been a terrific interlude but I must now concentrate on the cricket ahead.

Team meetings on tour are not all about cricket and today Bob Bennett advised all the players not to stray too far from the hotel and preferably not to go out alone. There have been a number of incidents on the beach-front outside the hotel and there is a faintly uncomfortable atmosphere about the place. The hotel manager advised us to stay inside for our New Year celebrations and Bob Bennett has organised a team meal and party for tomorrow night. We have a practice session on New Year's Eve and the game against Durban starts the next day.

31 December
New Year celebrations courtesy of the TCCB but mixed emotions for me as many of the other players are accompanied by their wives but my family is back in Cape Town. I had an interesting discussion with Dominic Cork on the benefit of our good team performances and how this might assist our individual ambitions to play at the highest level. Seeing him bat in the nets makes me feel like taking him to one side and talking to him about batting as he has tremendous potential. He can show arrogance on the field but this is not part of his personality away from the game. I was unsure whether we would get on with each other on tour, and he felt the same way. Touring does give you an opportunity to get to know other players in a way impossible on the county circuit at home, and I am pleased that our reservations about each other proved to be unfounded.

Although it is not always my place to do so, I have this feeling inside to assist young players realise their potential. I think it's probably because I feel, looking back, that I was never given that sort of progressive tuition as a young professional in my early days at Sussex. I didn't receive the help I needed and I feel passionately that young players need help to overcome the insecurity and occasional despair you experience as a young batsman. If you have a mentor to talk you through these difficulties then you feel your skills and character are developing in a progressive way. It is only in recent years that I have been the recipient of this sort of guidance, from David Smith and Norman Gifford in particular. John Barclay has also helped me with certain things. One of the positive aspects of this tour, being a senior player, has been an opportunity to talk to players like Dominic Cork, not only about technique but also about the mental approach to batting.

1 January 1994 - Natal at Kingsmead, first day

Not a good start to the new year. We won the toss and elected to bowl on a wicket which we misread. Martin Bicknell returned from injury but he broke down in his fourth over, in obvious pain, and I feel very sorry for him as it looks like the end of his tour. We didn't take our first wicket until just before tea by which time they had almost 200 on the board. It was an essential learning experience for the team, as it is the first time we have been under any serious pressure. Along with Hugh Morris, John Crawley and Mark Lathwell I dropped a catch, but managed to hold on to one at silly point to deny the opener his maiden first-class century. Generally we had a difficult day in the field in steaming humidity. A team meeting in the evening confirmed that Martin Bicknell will be returning home and this sad news ended what had been a pretty miserable day for the team. He will be replaced by Paul Taylor who will join the party in Pretoria.

2 January - Natal, second day

We failed to bowl them out as we had hoped and they made 458 for nine before declaring. We lost a couple of wickets early on and Hugh Morris and myself, with interruptions for bad light, managed to see it through to the close. I spent the evening on one of my duties as a county captain, writing my annual article for the 1994 edition of the Sussex handbook. Most of it concerns the peaks and troughs of the Nat West trophy; the joy of winning the semi-final and the desolation at losing the final on the last ball. There was little space to elaborate on the other major issues of the season, such as the retirement of Adrian Jones, releasing Tony Pigott and Brad Donelan. The decision on Lester was particularly hard as he is a personal friend, and I found it difficult to approach him after he had received the news. I regret not speaking to him earlier.

Contract meetings at the end of the season can be traumatic. The captain and cricket manager have to make tough decisions which are then discussed and approved by the committee. The secretary and manager then discuss the situation with the players concerned and it can be a painful time. Not all players are re-engaged when their contracts end, and some take the opportunity to move on if the opportunity presents itself and the county is prepared to make them available. The TCCB circulates two lists of players; one for players not available and the other for players whose counties will not prevent their release even though they might be under contract. Last year was a watershed in other ways as my brother Colin, with whom I have played cricket my whole career, decided to move on to Derbyshire.

3 January - Natal, third day

What a day! Without question the most disappointing day of the tour so far. All out for 116 on a wicket so flat that Malcolm Marshall was reduced to bowling off-spin off a two-step run-up. We were undone by feeling the pressure of a big score against us, coupled with some dreadful batting. After being dropped off a loose shot I scrambled a single and from the safety of the bowler's end rebuked myself for losing concentration. I just couldn't generate my normal positive attitude, my mind was all over the place, and I was judged leg-before soon after. We followed on and I felt inexplicably nervous going in to bat. After a reasonable start, I started to feel more positive and decided to play my natural game against the spinners, which is to hit them over the top and dominate. I ran down the wicket to a ball which wasn't there to drive and instead of blocking it, I literally chipped it to a mid-on who was deep enough to run a single to, had I hit it along the ground. I walked off feeling embarrassed that I could ever be a contender for Test cricket having played a shot like that. Thirty minutes on the dressing room floor with a towel over my head didn't make me feel any better. I was so disappointed with myself that I felt as if all the runs I had ever scored counted for nothing at that moment. I'm normally philosophical about dismissals but this one really hurt. I telephoned Melanie who managed to reassure me that I hadn't turned into the worst player in England with one horrendous shot.

4 January - Natal, final day
I didn't expect to be back in my hotel room early afternoon but we were bowled out for 285 and lost heavily by an innings and 57 runs. We were out-played by a weakened Natal side, and Malcolm Marshall didn't even take a wicket. We know how badly we performed and feel determined to show our character and bounce back against Northern Transvaal. The press reaction was typical, with one reporter, Bill Day, asking if this performance is what we have come to expect from an England side and saying *"Does this show the doubts you've always had in your mind about the batting?"* No surprise really given we had won eight matches in a row!

7 January - Northern Transvaal at Centurion Park, first day
We lost the toss but bowled superbly to dismiss them for 138. Mark Ilott and Martin McCague took four for 32 and three for 34 respectively. Overnight we were 81 for four on a difficult pitch. I had earlier woken up with an extremely stiff neck and although I could field I had to move down the batting order as I couldn't turn to face what was proving to be a fierce seam attack.

8 January - Northern Transvaal, second day
Hugh Morris batted exceptionally well for 57 and Mal Loye hit 40. I managed 11 and we ended with 205 and a well-earned lead of 67. Although it would appear that

we are on top, our opponents have been inspired by South Africa's dramatic second-Test win against Australia and the locals are hoping they can repeat the dose against us. We had them 75 for seven in the second innings, a lead of only eight, but an eighth-wicket partnership of 74 runs between Rudi Bryson and Steve Elworthy helped them to 162, a lead of 95 and something to bowl at. We came off early due to bad light, needing a further 91 to win and all wickets intact.

In reflective mood I considered the frustrations of not being in charge on the field. I remember when I took over the captaincy at Sussex, Norman Gifford said to me that once you have been captain for a while there is no way you want to go back to not having that control and responsibility. When I disagree with Hugh Morris over team selection or whatever, I don't force my views on him, as I respect his position as captain of the team, but it can be frustrating not to have authority on the field.

9 January - Northern Transvaal, third day

We won the game just before lunch and I was really pleased with the way I played. Even though I've faced hostile bowling in my career, one particular delivery I received from Steve Elworthy will stay in my memory for a long time. He wasn't bowling particularly quickly but he banged this ball in just back off a length and it obviously hit one of the cracks. It flew straight over my head at an alarming pace and my eyes were transfixed following the trajectory. It almost cleared the keeper's outstretched arm above his head.

45

After the game we had a discussion about our fielding which has let us down on occasions. It is easier to discuss flaws following a victory when lessons can be learned in a progressive and constructive way, rather than in the form of a negatively based post-mortem in the wake of a defeat. Our inability to field well is amazing given that we are a young side and although I hate to say what it was like when I first started out and so on I couldn't help but mention to a couple of the guys that I can't understand a reluctance to enjoy fielding. My first game for Sussex was a Sunday League game against Lancashire in 1981 and I batted at ten. At that stage I travelled with the first team as twelfth man, solely for my fielding ability, and John Barclay decided to put me in the side for my fielding. As a youngster on the staff, to spend time with experienced players such as Garth le Roux, Imran Khan, John Barclay, Geoff Arnold, Ian Grieg, Chris Waller and Paul Phillipson was an essential part of my cricketing education. Some young players look on being twelfth man as a real chore, but if they adopt a positive attitude and use the experience to learn, then this will benefit them when it comes to forcing a way into the first-team.

I also had a productive discussion with Mark Lathwell, Adrian Dale and John Crawley about why a negative attitude enveloped the team in Durban. We agreed that there was an inevitability about the poor performance against Natal and I made a mental note to watch for these signs in the forthcoming domestic season, and act sooner rather than later.

11 January

Travelled to Kimberley where tomorrow we have a one-day game against Griqualand West. This evening we had a team selection meeting: Bob Bennett (who sits in and listens), Wayne Morton, Phil Neale, Hugh Morris and myself. I welcomed the opportunity to suggest that we approach the last leg of the tour with a view to the Test match and give some of the bowlers batting practice, without affecting the balance in any detrimental way. Phil Neale was of a different opinion, and was not receptive to any suggestion which in his view might jeopardise our prospects of winning the remaining games. I could be a casualty of my own initiative as, although I am the only player to have played in every game, I could be asked to make way tomorrow.

12 January - Griqualand West at Kimberley

We won easily against an inferior side. We batted first and scored 216 in 50 overs on a very slow wicket. Robert Croft and Dominic Cork moved up the order and put on a good partnership of over 100. I played after all and came in at seven, with just a few overs to go. In reply they fell well short. Now it's on to Bloemfontein to face Orange Free State, captained by Franklyn Stephenson, the Sussex all-rounder. I am really looking forward to this game as he'll be trying to get me out and there's no way I'll let it happen!

13 January

A very interesting day in many ways, as it is our first

day in Bloemfontein and there are the first signs of tension creeping into the camp, with just a couple of weeks to go to the end of the tour. An end-of-term feeling is in the air and we need to keep our minds on the cricket. At the team meeting, Bob Bennett reiterated that we are making history as an England touring side, winning ten out of eleven games and there is no reason why it won't be thirteen out of fourteen at the end of the tour. Keith Fletcher has conveyed a message through Bob Bennett that our achievements will benefit English cricket as a whole, especially with the West Indies tour coming up. It's worth noting that the tour manager has been faultless in organising every detail of the tour. He has read the mood of the players so well and this has clearly contributed to our success on the field.

14 January - Orange Free State at Springbok Park, first day

We lost the toss and Orange Free State, the Castle Cup holders, batted on a slow and low wicket. Thanks to four wickets from Martin McCague and some hard work in the field on a very hot day, they finished on 344 for nine, losing Franklyn Stephenson for 46 in the last over of the day. The aim tomorrow is to bat well and amass a useful total.

Robert Croft and Mark Ilott entertained us all in the evening. I have a small video camera and I asked them to film the ground, do a few interviews and so on. They ended up doing an extremely funny parody of the TV show *Through the Keyhole*, as if hosted by Richie Benaud.

Mark Ilott did a great impression of Lloyd Grossman and instead of the usual *"Who would live in a house like this?"* it was *"Who would carry a cricket coffin around like this?"* They then proceeded to take the mickey out of a few of the guys and added some much needed light relief to help dispel the niggle creeping into the dressing room during the closing stages of the tour.

15 January - Orange Free State, second day

Shades of our failure against Natal. They managed another 26 runs for the last wicket to reach a good total of 370. In reply we lost a couple of early wickets, including Mark Lathwell for a duck. He is having a really bad time at the moment, is lacking in confidence and feeling the pressure of being exposed to Test cricket, by his own admission, before he was ready. The press are on to him out here and he deserves time and support to get through this bad patch. At this stage of his career his talent should be nurtured, but he is being exposed in a way which could prove to be detrimental to him and to England.

We were soon four for two and under a lot of pressure. I made 53 and much to my annoyance and to the bowler's delight chipped one to mid-wicket off Franklyn Stephenson. The wicket played low and they bowled to a disciplined line outside off-stump which made it very difficult for us. Mal Loye showed his impetuosity when he raced down the wicket to the off-spinner and was stumped attempting a sweep. Steve Rhodes was bowled attempting to pull a full toss. In my opinion, Mal is making the sort of mistakes we all make in our first year of professional cricket, and he shouldn't really be in a position where he has to learn the craft of first-class batting on an England A tour. It is unfair and could actually hold him back as he is really feeling the pressure of having to perform to justify his inclusion. It doesn't help that his coach at home is also the coach on tour, Phil Neale - Mal might benefit from being able to turn to someone else when things go wrong.

Phil Neale is obviously disappointed and is taking a very harsh and negative view of what is only our second bad day in seven weeks of cricket. At times he seems to forget how hard the game is. He is keen for us to bat for time, to eradicate the bad shots which have cost wickets, but I argue the case for us to bat something closer to our natural game. Of course, bat with caution when the situation demands it, but generally it is better to play to your strengths. Your purpose has to be clear in your mind when you go out to bat and it's a struggle if you fall between the two stools of batting for time and playing your natural game. To find the right balance between adapting your batting to suit a specific situation, such as avoiding a follow-on, and playing a natural run-scoring game, is a lot to ask young players. It is not always constructive to negatively criticise them for not exercising the type of judgement which comes only through the one thing they don't yet have to add to their promise and skills - experience. There is no conflict between us, just a difference of opinion.

It was a surprise when Franklyn Stephenson failed

to enforce the follow-on. We are still in contention and should at least save the game.

16 January - Orange Free State, third day
They batted on today to declare at 262 for nine, one hour after tea, leaving us a target of 453 to win. It was roasting hot in the field and we spent the day operating a policy of containment. After the penultimate over we had reached 50 without loss; then came the last over. The left-arm spinner bowled into the rough, Lathwell failed to get his pad in the way and was bowled behind his legs. As I watched from the balcony all I could think about was what a lonely game cricket can be. At that moment nobody else in the team could have felt as low as Mark Lathwell. Paul Taylor went in as nightwatchman and one over-ambitious drive later we were two down. A tough day ahead, but with guts and determination we'll rise to the challenge.

The evening was as hot as the cricket. Franklyn Stephenson hosted a barbecue and, accompanied by Wayne Morton on guitar, we had a good sing-song and relaxed in preparation for tomorrow.

17 January - Orange Free State, final day
Thanks to the brilliance of John Crawley and some solid support from the other batsmen, we managed to save the game. What I like about John Crawley is his even temperament, responsibility and maturity in defeat and victory. It is so uncommon in such a young player and sets him apart as a prospect for the future. I shared a partnership of over 100 with him and scored 46 before

chancing a single and being run-out by a stunning direct hit from mid-off. At one stage we were looking as if we could go for a win but the game petered out to a draw with us 131 runs behind with 14 overs remaining.

We went into this game with four-and-a-bit bowlers, on a flat wicket. One of the bowlers, Paul Taylor, has only just arrived and in my view our bowling options were restricted by our selection. I strongly believe that you need bowling options to win matches on this sort of wicket, and you must depend on the top five batsmen to score sufficient runs. It is the first time on this tour I've really disagreed over selection before a game.

After the disaster in Durban, it was a good achievement to bat under pressure for a whole day, and hopefully this will be recognised by the England management at home.

21 January - Border at East London, first day

We won the toss and decided to bat on what looked like a good wicket. John Crawley and Hugh Morris got off to a brisk start, then Hugh was run-out and Adrian Dale came in at three. Mark Lathwell was left out due to his lack of form and, more crucially, his complete loss of confidence. I came in at 59 for two and was out lbw to a slower ball from Fourie. Mal Loye and Steve Rhodes put the show back on the road by grinding out the runs and concentrating on staying at the crease. Mal's innings of 71 was very patient and restrained, which no doubt pleased Phil Neale. In one passage of play their occasional slow left-armer bowled 10 overs without conceding a run, such was the pace of our progress. By the end of the day we reached 229 for six.

I was very disappointed with my batting today. Again, I felt too negative and lacked the belligerence I thrive on. I'm not sure why, but the anxiety of wanting to finish the tour on a high note is obviously a factor.

22 January - Border, second day
We ended up with 320, thanks to a good century from Steve Rhodes. It was an unexciting day's play, with runs hard to get on a dead wicket, and by the close they had replied with 125 for four.

23 January - Border, third day
Today we took their last six wickets in one session before lunch, to take a first-innings lead of 120. I went to the wicket with a much more positive approach, knowing that we wanted to build on our lead and leave enough time to bowl them out to win the game. I was out for 46, hooking a ball which was too wide and too high. I've had my chances to score more than the one century so far and will be going all out to put that right in the Test match.

24 January - Border, final day
Today we were ultimately frustrated by the loss of play to rain. We set Border 296 to win in what became 77 overs, and they held on for a draw despite the fact we had almost five overs at the last-wicket pair. Hugh Morris is doing an excellent job keeping the players'

motivation levels high in preparation for the Test match. He is very adept at talking to the team between breaks of play to set out the strategy for the next session and to keep everyone's mind on the game. I tend not to do this too much at Hove, unless I feel it is particularly relevant. Obviously, I do speak to the players a lot, but less so when we are batting. This is something I can learn from Hugh as he reads the game so well, is very approachable and a good communicator.

26 January

The next task is to pick eleven from thirteen to play the Test match, with the added problem of having lost Dominic Cork who has had to return home on compassionate grounds. The selection meeting decided to exclude Martin McCague and Paul Taylor, leaving us with two spinners, and Mark Lathwell as the extra batsman. The wicket looks very flat and the extra batting power will be important, with the spinners exploiting any turn from the rough as the match progresses. Personally, I'm really looking forward to the Test and it means a lot to me to represent an official England side for the first time in a five-day Test. I feel relaxed and ready to play my natural game, so I'm not putting myself under any pressure.

27 January - South Africa A at St George's Park, first day

We had a great day although we lost the toss and they decided to bat. They started well, and reached 81 without loss at lunch, but our bowlers applied the pressure, the field sat back, and we stuck at it on a very hot day to restrict them to 173 for four. In the last session we bowled 28 overs for 40 runs and took three wickets.

28 January - South Africa A, second day

We broke through early on with the wickets of Adrian Kuiper and Steve Palframan, but Crookes and Simons took the attack to our spinners and put together a partnership of 73. Heads started to go down a little, but we stuck at it and they reached 357. We had hoped to see the day through without losing a wicket, but unfortunately Mark Lathwell's dismal run continued when he was out in the first over without scoring. I felt so sorry for him and I know he just can't wait to return home and put the tour behind him. John Crawley was next out, for 29, and we ended the day on 54 for two.

29 January - South Africa A, third day

Three controversial dismissals, including my own, in the last half-hour spoilt a great day. I went out to bat at 63 for three, which became 92 for four and brought Mal Loye to the crease. We added 171 in 67 overs and were together until the final 30 minutes. Mal played patiently and his shot selection demonstrated the progress he has made during this tour. I was given out lbw in the last over of the day to a ball which the bowler later admitted was clearly moving down the leg side. I scored 130 and played my most responsible innings of the tour.

I set out determined to finish the tour with a big score, and when I arrived at the ground this morning I had a very clear picture in my mind of the bowling I was likely to face and how I would deal with it. My mental preparation last night was thorough. I reminded myself that I have scored over 30 first-class centuries, and replayed innings in my head to be ready for today. When you make a big score you are enclosed in a cocoon of concentration. I find it hard to recall particular shots from major innings, and tend to dwell more on scoring nought than 100. I was determined to score runs and what I considered to be an average tour has now moved up to good, but I'm still frustrated at losing my wicket in the last over. The odd umpiring mistake is part of the game and genuine errors are made in all walks of life. As a professional cricketer you learn to take the rough with the smooth.

30 January - South Africa A, fourth day
Our innings finished today at 329, just 28 behind. They started positively but never looked like breaking out to set any sort of target for us. There is very little in the wicket and run scoring is not easy by any means. Jimmy Cook fell at 48 and overnight they are 156 for three. Our best hope at the start of the day was to sneak 10 wickets!

31 January - South Africa A, final day
Unfortunately the game we hoped we might have didn't materialise. We bowled them out just before lunch for 221, thanks to a five-wicket haul from Mark

Ilott, leaving us exactly 250 to win. Mark Ilott has had a remarkable tour, finishing with nine wickets in this game and a total of 37 in only six first-class games. We lost early wickets, and Mark Lathwell endured another setback but I'm confident he'll learn from this experience and become a better player for it. In some respects you have to go through really bad patches to improve your game, and when you come through a poor spell the experience helps you come out the other side intact next time round.

Mal Loye and myself enjoyed another good partnership and I finished on 45 not out. Once out for 175 runs has not done my England chances any harm and I'll be at the other end of the telephone should a call come through from the West Indies. The fines kitty provided the necessary funds for an excellent night out, and we reflected on a very successful tour.

The tour itself has exceeded all our expectations, with ten wins out of fourteen matches, and only one defeat. Hugh Morris did a really good job as captain. Phil Neale is enthusiastic, meticulous, and is obviously coping well with the adjustment from playing in a side to managing one. I've no doubt that his admirable professionalism will stand him in good stead. Bob Bennett was faultless, and a pleasure to observe in action.

Before the tour I set myself a target of at least 500 runs for the tour and an average of over 40. Thanks to the Port Elizabeth Test, I managed to exceed my expectations with a total of 593 runs, a highest score of 130, two centuries, and an average of almost 54. One element of the tour I had not anticipated was thinking too negatively about my batting. At home I have David Smith and Norman Gifford to pat me on the back and motivate me, and on this tour I missed their influence. All players, whether accomplished, young or experienced, occasionally need guidance and motivation from those around them.

Pre-season trip to Malaga

This is my third year of captaincy and I feel a lot more relaxed about the forthcoming season than I have in the last couple of years. At times in the last two seasons I was a bit uptight when things didn't go well and players didn't do what I wanted them to do. With experience, I've learned that there are difficult situations to deal with, and the frustrations that come with captaining a county represent another challenge in the search for success. The basic disciplines that Giffy and myself expect from the team are now in place, and there is less need to constantly remind the players of what we expect. It is interesting that we are sitting back a lot more this year on the fundamental points which have taken a couple of seasons to instil in the team, not that we would be slow to reiterate a point should it be necessary. The idea is to create an environment where the players can relax, build confidence, and play their natural game free of the stifling fear of failure. I want to achieve the right blend of discipline and freedom to allow the team and individuals to flourish.

From a team point of view, with Jarv having joined us, the ability I see in the side should allow us to challenge for every competition. There is no reason in my mind why this shouldn't be the case. That we have the ability is not in doubt, and as Eddie Hemmings said to me, what we now need is a belief that we can win something, and it is up to Giffy and myself to instil this self-belief in individuals and therefore the team. One of the major lessons we learned last year, demonstrated by reaching the Nat West final, was that we can beat the best sides. To be one ball away from winning a trophy was at the time a crushing blow, but the experience has contributed to the confidence and self-belief we need to go one better this season. I need to communicate this message before we start playing games. We ended last season on a high and need to carry this through.

From a personal point of view, my ambition to play for England is as strong as ever. I do feel that unless I have another successful season this year, my chance could evaporate. I was told when I returned from South Africa that there had been a question on the BBC programme Question of Sport . . . *"Who has a first-class average of over 50 for the last five seasons, scoring over 7500 runs, but has yet to play a Test match for his country?"* The answer? Alan Wells. That is an aggregate of 1500 runs a season, over five seasons, and I occasionally think to myself how can I keep doing that year after year without the reward I feel is justified. There must come a time when it is hard to keep motivating yourself, when you realise that no matter what you do the ultimate recognition is missing. I'm no quitter, and I'll play as hard this year as in any other. I can't help thinking, looking at the middle-order falling apart in the West Indies time after time, that I could be there using my skills and experience, batting and fighting for my country. Speaking to Neil Lenham tonight, I likened it to enduring the frustration of playing in a county second-team, scoring runs all over the place, and wondering why you are not given a chance to step up to a first-team which is losing games time after time.

Nothing will effect my motivation to do well for Sussex, and if I score another 1500 runs and get picked for England then I'll treat it as an unexpected bonus. The game itself and Sussex are too important for anything to seriously hamper my desire to do well for myself and my county.

During the pre-season trip I forced myself to watch our innings in the Nat West final. Whilst I was batting, David Gower was commentating and he mentioned that we had a chat in Portsmouth when I sought his advice on dealing with the pressure of needing to keep scoring runs to stay in the frame for the West Indies tour. Gower told me that on the many occasions when he was under pressure to score runs to be selected for England, he tended to fail. Relax, switch off the pressure, and play your natural game was his advice. This really helped at the time and it helped me focus and finish the season strongly. There is a lot of self-inflicted pressure in cricket. It is something that is with you throughout your career, whether as a youngster feeling the pressure of trying to stay on the staff, to a capped professional endeavouring to keep churning out the runs, or wickets. When you are young and making your way in the game you don't know yourself that well, and you don't know what the game's all about, so you feel external pressures. Whereas when you are in control of yourself and familiar with the day to day stresses and strains of professional cricket, the pressures tend to be self-inflicted. Watching Robin Smith go out to bat in the West Indies, I could see and sense, from his pumped-up state, his determination to score runs, but he did not look in control of himself, and the combination of facing the bowling, poor form and an anxious state of mind was too much to overcome. The key to a successful season for me is to relax, retain a positive attitude, stay focused, and play to my strengths.

14 April

Back from the pre-season trip to a wet and cold England. We had a practice in the middle at the ground today and Jarv looked every bit a class bowler. Ed Giddins has impressed, although he is often reluctant to extend himself and can be a lazy character in need of a boot up the backside, to which he responds positively. One of the reasons for Giddo's new found application is the signing of Jason Lewry, a young left-arm seamer who has been playing local league cricket for Goring. He has good pace, a smooth action, brings the ball in to the right-hander and impressed many of the senior players both in Spain and in the middle today. At 22 he is a late arrival, but Ian Gould and John Barclay were not slow to spot his talent when he appeared in a friendly with the MCC at Arundel. When he came for a trial, his run up was not much more than a few steps around the wicket, a legacy of playing indoor cricket for England. Although he is being thrown in at the deep end, he has the confidence to succeed.

I'm looking forward to the first game of the season, against Scotland in the Benson & Hedges. Traditionally Sussex have been bad starters and this is something I want to overcome this year, so it is important we get off to a good start against Gloucestershire in the first championship game. I'm looking for a good start for Sussex and a good start for Alan Wells.

My playing season proper starts in a game against Middlesex for England A. There's nothing on the game apart from personal pride and trying to impress the England selectors early on!

19 April

Today we had a friendly match against Gloucestershire and it helped me focus my mind on captaining the team in the season ahead. Pre-season is all about thinking and talking cricket rather than playing, so it was a tonic to concentrate solely on the game in hand. Martin Speight smacked the ball to all parts and Jason Lewry bowled really well.

I'm becoming tired of the butcher, baker and candlestick-maker telling me that I should be in the England side. It's not that I don't appreciate an encouraging word, but at the moment it's driving me crazy. I'd be happier for people to realise that I'm not playing for England and that it is up to me to keep going in order to be picked. Hugh Morris is injured at the moment and Phil Neale telephoned to inform me I have the honour of captaining England A at Lords against Middlesex.

25 April

The team atmosphere for England A against Middlesex was as good as it was in South Africa, although the match was a bit of a non-event as Gatting seemed to hog the game with 58 in the first innings and over 200 not out in the second. It was a real pleasure to captain the side, and after we batted well in the first innings we made Middlesex follow-on, but the game eventually fizzled out to a draw. Gatting gave us a target on the final afternoon of 200 in 20 overs to give his bowlers some practice.

A few issues are on my mind as we start the season proper. I am confident the team knows what is expected from them in the one-day match tomorrow. I'll reiterate the basics just before the game begins, and during play if necessary. I need to talk to Billy Athey about his role in one-day cricket. I want him to be far more positive in his batting and I'm happy for the side to bat around David Smith, who is less happy to smash the ball around early in an innings. Billy can be more aggressive and at times last year he was too circumspect against ordinary bowling. I also want to talk to Ian Salisbury about his championship bowling, having noticed in the West Indies that as soon as he came on to bowl, he had a deep mid-wicket and a deep cover, which is far too defensive and is basically setting the field for a bad ball. I don't want that, and although we might have words, as Sals is strong-headed and at times a bit of a know-all on field placing, he has to learn to listen to myself and Giffy.

After the relative peace of the pre-season build-up, today was hectic. Press day is a seemingly endless round of interviews with the media, team photographs, individual photographs, sponsors' photographs and so on. We enjoy a good relationship with the local press and the players are happy to give up their time to talk with sports reporters. It is founded on mutual trust and respect, and as long as the media are not out to get you, there is no reason not to enjoy a good working relationship with them. The Sunday League is a good example, when local radio will invite players to accompany the commentator for a short period. After all the posing comes a meeting with Giffy and Chris Waller to talk about the team for tomorrow, then on with the pads for a practice session in the middle.

The team feels confident and ready for the first game. Confident enough to check the odds on us winning a competition this year. Last year we were 150 to 1 to win the championship, so we put £500 from the players' pool on ourselves. This year we are 100 to 1, which I think is generous in the extreme, so perhaps we'll have another flutter.

26 April - Scotland at Hove, Benson & Hedges

The start of the season with a Benson & Hedges game against Scotland at Hove. It couldn't have gone any better, the only thing we did wrong was lose the toss. We bowled well, restricting them to 157 in 55 overs, then knocked off the runs in 40 overs for the loss of two wickets.

I made it clear to the team before the game that I was looking for a disciplined and professional performance, and everything went according to plan without a hint of complacency. We have so many players out there who have played a lot of cricket, and one aspect which did please me was that I didn't have to shout to keep them in position or change a field setting. It is easier to concentrate on the game in hand when the players watch the captain and can be moved without the need to constantly attract their attention by bawling across the ground.

Before the game we were toying with team selection, particularly whether to play Ed Giddins or not as he has some problems at the moment. I was concerned that both Giddo and the rest of the team would not be distracted by any outside issues, so I had him in the office yesterday to spell out exactly what is expected of him. It was necessary to be heavy-handed but I'm not prepared to let players step out of line. All credit to Giddo as he responded very positively today, with good preparation before the game coupled with a sharp performance in the field. It's important to keep reminding him of his duties towards the team and to himself.

I managed to discuss with Billy Athey this morning his approach to one-day cricket, and he had been reflecting on this over the winter. I explained that I want him to be far more positive and aggressive, and leave the anchor role to David Smith. The next discussion with a player has to be with Sals. He bowled nowhere near well enough today, conceding nearly five runs an over compared with well under three for the other bowlers.

When batting, I felt relaxed and comfortable, not going at the ball too hard, waiting for the bad ball and despatching it from the middle of the bat to the boundary. I was pleased with the rhythm of my innings and felt 'quiet' at the crease - a word often used by Giffy to describe batting without forcing and tension.

There is a tangible sense of expectation and excitement for the pleasures of the familiar routine which develops as the season progresses. Even though I've been there many times, the start of the season is a special time when you begin to hope that all the preparation and hard work will pay off. Our next game is a championship match against Gloucestershire, but before that we have a couple of one-day friendly matches against Kent and Middlesex, which coincide with a second-eleven game at Hove. The players have the option, especially the batsmen, to spend more meaningful time in the middle, so along with four or five others I'll be playing with the seconds this week.

28 April

Watching Sals being interviewed on TV last night triggered off the discussion I was expecting. Both myself and the manager were not happy with what he had to say and the way he said it. He sounded annoyed and arrogantly demanded to know exactly what was expected of him: wickets, or to bowl tightly and keep the runs down. He didn't sound like the Sals we know, and had a dig at the press and selectors, so I thought it would be a good idea to retire to the captain's room for a chat. Giffy handled the situation calmly and constructively. He made it clear that it was time to stop playing the Test player's charade, and that the arrogance and know-it-all attitude, never present in

Sals' game and character a few years ago, had to be checked. Deep down Sals knows that he is not being completely honest with himself, and the anxiety he feels over his poor form is manifesting itself in an uncharacteristic fashion.

During lunch against Scotland he had questioned my intent to curtail his bowling spell, seemingly ignorant of the fact that he was the most expensive bowler on the field! There was a time when he would have apologised for going for so many runs against mediocre opposition and accepted my decision without a murmur. Now he's a Test bowler it's as if he is suddenly immune to bowling badly. Inwardly he knows that he has bowled badly, but he really needs to open up and be prepared to acknowledge it outwardly too, for the good of his game and for the team. Phil Edmonds is a good example of a bowler who completely lost his action and confidence, yet he was brave enough and determined enough to go back to basics and put things right. Sals needs to keep working at his game, to see county cricket as his bread and butter, and enjoy the bonus of Test cricket when he earns it. Our session together gave me an opportunity to tell him that he couldn't have the field placings he enjoyed in the West Indies: no deep mid-wicket and deep cover as soon as he comes on to bowl, as a false insurance against the bad ball. Over-protective fields might help the individual bowler's figures, but in my view it conceals poor bowling. If he gets hit then it will be highlighted and the bowler will realise that he needs to work to prevent the ball being smacked over mid-wicket, rather than post the fielder deeper to mask a deficiency. We told Sals that we need him to bowl well for Sussex, and the chat helped him clear his mind and realise that we will support him in every way to improve his game. The discussion was constructive throughout and I'm sure that Sals will reflect over the weekend and return next week with a new attitude.

A story Giffy tells is that within six weeks of playing Test cricket, he was on the field with the Worcestershire second-eleven - he has experienced the highs and lows of professional cricket first-hand. This is one of the reasons why he is able to handle Sals so well, and it is so valuable for young players to have an opportunity to learn from this depth of knowledge and experience.

30 April
Captaining the second-eleven presented a good opportunity to observe the players: Jason Lewry bowled well, taking three wickets in one over; Danny Law did well although he was a touch inconsistent; a young lad called James Curtly impressed me, as he did in the pre-season trip, particularly with his enthusiasm. The game itself did not provide the sort of practice I was looking for, and I should have taken Giffy's advice and watched the cricket instead. However, it made me realise that compared to other counties, we have some promising talent at Sussex, and some young players not far off challenging for a first-team place.

In the friendly match against Middlesex at Uxbridge, we needed two to win off the last two balls, but the game ended in a tie! It was good to see Keith Greenfield score a hundred, and really demonstrates the strength in depth at the club. It is up to me and the first-team to set the standards and lay the foundation for the talented young players to build on in the future.

1 May
I captained the Duchess of Norfolk's team today against New Zealand at Arundel. We bowled and fielded reasonably well and at tea Paul Parker and myself were still in, needing 140-odd in 30 overs. I was yorked after tea and we collapsed soon afterwards. Nevertheless it was an enjoyable game with only professional pride at stake!

I've been reading the press reports about Graham Gooch announcing his willingness to tour with England again, and therefore walking into the Test side for the summer. I resolved to work twice as hard and score twice as many runs.

4 May
Travelled down to Bristol this afternoon after a brief practice session at Hove. We are all raring to go in our opening championship match, against Gloucestershire. Courtney Walsh has continued his good form from the West Indies and we'll need to work hard to keep him out. Personally I'm looking forward to facing Walsh as he's always a challenge. Jamie Hall missed the trip and we've brought Jason Lewry down with us. It won't do Ed Giddins any harm to be looking over his shoulder at the youngster waiting in the wings. I spent some time with Jamie before I left the ground and reassured

him that he will feature in our plans, but for the time being he has to score runs with the second-team and be ready to take his chance when the time comes. Last season he failed to seize his chance to cement a first-team place, but he appears to be ready this year.

5 May - Gloucestershire at Bristol, first day

The team-talk this morning concentrated on reiterating the need to play positive cricket and get off to a good start in the championship. We have been notoriously slow starters in the last few seasons and I feel that this is the year to put it right. Although we lost play to rain, we had them 64 for four by the end of play. After winning the toss, Courtney asked us to bowl, which was what I wanted to do anyway. All the seamers bowled well, ably supported by an excellent performance behind the stumps by Peter Moores.

Ian Salisbury has returned from a weekend away and seems to be back to his old self again which is great to see. We've already selected the side for Sunday, and Keith Greenfield will be joining us on Saturday then staying with the party to go up to Trent Bridge to play Notts in the B & H.

6 May - Gloucestershire, second day

After all our hopes of a good start, Gloucestershire took control today with a good partnership between Jack Russell, no doubt motivated by Steve Rhodes scoring a century for Worcestershire, and Chris Broad. They were still together at the end of the day. The wicket dried out and the bowlers worked hard to extract something from a flat track. We thought we had Chris Broad out early in his innings when a ball which hit the back of his glove after striking him on the thigh pad was well caught by Martin Speight close in. Unfortunately the umpire at the other end didn't see it, but I felt Trevor Jesty, standing at square-leg, must have seen and heard it, but it was not to be. From a potential 70-odd for six they ended on 256 for five. Sals bowled better but needs a rest from the Sunday side, as he doesn't need the pressure of batsmen slogging him in a limited-over thrash until he's found his rhythm in the four-day game. Franklyn Stephenson is more motivated than I have ever seen him at the start of a season. He's such a big player for us in every respect, and it's terrific for team spirit that he is so enthusiastic about our prospects.

7 May - Gloucestershire, third day
They declared at 319 and got off to a reasonable start before it all went horribly wrong for us. Billy Athey went to hospital for stitches after being struck on the side of the face by a return from Alleyne, and David Smith retired hurt when he was hit on the thumb. Neil Lenham batted well for 42 and I was out, for 51, hooking Walsh who bowled with real fire taking five for 66. We lost the last six wickets for a mere 28 runs, narrowly avoiding the follow-on by nine. By the end of the day Gloucestershire compiled a lead of 180, losing two wickets in the process to Ed Giddins in an impressive spell backing up Jarv and Franklyn.

We're good enough to win the 40-over slog

tomorrow and a good performance will help lift us for the final day on Monday.

8 May - Gloucestershire, Sunday League

One hour before the start we told Sals that he wasn't in the team today and he was clearly disappointed, reminding me that he has never let us down in one-day cricket. Although he disagreed, he accepted the decision pretty well. We won the toss and batted. The slow start was not what I wanted, especially after our discussions about taking a more positive and aggressive approach. I scored 61, breaking my best bat in the process, with excellent support from Martin Speight who hit 56. Neil Lenham kept the runs coming with an unbeaten 58. Without Chris Broad and Courtney Walsh they never looked like winning and fell 46 short of our 233.

Eddie Hemmings played in place of Sals, and with him and Franklyn I had the usual differences of opinion over field placings. Both are experienced cricketers and they can be adamant about what they want when bowling. Afterwards in the changing room I felt the need to remind them that, although I'm ready to listen to suggestions, there is only one captain on the field, and that's me. Mike Gatting has a similar situation for Middlesex. Embers will often move his field here and there, and Gatt just moves the fielders back to where he wants them!

9 May - Gloucestershire, final day

We were looking forward to a run-chase today after

reducing Gloucestershire to 94 for eight before lunch. Luckless, we struggled to take the last two wickets and they added a match-saving 65 runs before declaring at 159, leaving us just under 300 to win in 50 overs. One bright spot was the performance of Peter Moores behind the stumps. He took eight catches in the match, which equalled his own Sussex record, jointly held with three others. Scoring six an over was never really on and the game petered out to a frustrating draw. Giffy pointed out that, faced with our strong batting line-up, Gloucestershire won't be the only county to shy away from us setting a realistic target this year. After the game it was off to a wet Nottingham to be ready for the B & H game tomorrow. I'm not sure on the side yet: it's unlikely I'll be playing two spinners - I might stick with Eddie Hemmings as long as he stops shouting at me!

10 May - Nottinghamshire at Trent Bridge, Benson & Hedges

After high hopes we were soundly beaten in the second round B & H match against Notts. Bill Athey and Martin Speight were out to long-hops; David Smith was stumped off a wide; Neil Lenham and myself had a rebuilding job to do but it was difficult to bat with any fluency, and any thoughts of posting a good total disappeared when we were both out in the same over. Thanks to some late resistance from Keith Greenfield and Paul Jarvis we hobbled along to an inadequate 239.

Franklyn had Paul Pollard caught at cover off a leading edge in his first over, then in the second

Crawley was brilliantly caught by Eddie Hemmings off Jarv. To see the oldest man on the circuit dive to his right at square-leg, to take a superb one-handed diving catch off the meat of the bat about two inches off the ground, was a remarkable sight. At 13 for two we were back in the game, or so we thought, until Tim Robinson and Jimmy Adams took control and ran away with it. Basically we were hammered. After a defeat there is always room for reflection on tactics and choice of players, and to think whether there is anything I could have done differently. It comes down to relying on eleven players to do their job properly, and if that doesn't happen then you lose. In one-day cricket our approach has been to play four specialist bowlers and two or three makeshift bowlers. It does beg the question whether it would be best to play five specialist bowlers in one-day games.

Sals was again left out and we travelled home together down the M1, which gave us a chance to talk about what he needs to do to get back into the one-day side. I still believe he needs to build his confidence by bowling good spells in four-day cricket before I'll expose him in the one-day slogs. He thinks otherwise, and feels that the constraints imposed by the one-day game actually help him find a good line and pace. I can understand his frustration and disappointment but at the moment he's not consistent enough to be risked.

Coming off the field at Notts I was told that the second-team had lost inside two days to Somerset, so all in all a bad few days for Sussex cricket, and no doubt one or two questions to be answered at the next committee meeting.

11 May

Hampshire tomorrow in our second championship match of the season. A couple of weeks ago I asked the groundsman to prepare a grassy, albeit dry grass, wicket to produce pace and bounce. It's been left dry for three weeks and has had a lot of grass rolled into it. I'd like the sort of wicket which Imran and Garth le Roux exploited so well in the early eighties, and it will be interesting to see how it turns out.

Thinking of players of the past, I spoke on the telephone today to Adrian Jones and Alan Green regarding ball-tampering and the Imran Khan bottle-top saga which has broken in the news. Even on a day off there is no respite from cricket in one form or another. I even heard today that my old headmaster and sportsmaster are trying to track me down to take part in some event. There's no shortage of requests like this, they come with the job really, and I always do my best to do what I can to help.

12 May - Hampshire at Hove, first day

Driving to the ground this morning, it feels more like the 12th of November with grey skies, cloud and rain. The wicket looks hard and grassy and has given us something to think about regarding team selection. Neil Lenham is struggling with a foot injury he picked up at the end of last season, and David Smith was at the ground yesterday having treatment on his back. After pinning up the team sheet, the only change being Jamie

Hall coming in for Neil Lenham, I had to have words with Keith Greenfield who felt aggrieved at not being in the side. He feels that he's first in line should a batsman be injured, but has let his enthusiasm and ambition, however laudable, get the better of him on this occasion by moaning through the grapevine instead of coming to me.

The start was delayed and we took the field after lunch. I won the toss, and having prepared a wicket for our bowlers, I chose to back up this policy by electing to bowl. The players seemed genuinely surprised at my decision and I must have looked worried because Speighty asked me if I was all right when I returned to the dressing room. It's some years since we prepared a wicket like this, and I explained to the team before the start that with our bowling potential now was the time to back it up. The last thing I wanted to hear was retrospective griping of the *"We should have batted"* variety. I demanded just hard work and professional application, even if it transpired that we should have batted first.

Franklyn bowled an absolute snorter in his first over which fizzed past Middleton's nose, clipped the outside edge, and was taken high above his head by Peter Moores. Jubilation. In his second over he bowled a similar ball, which if anything climbed even more steeply, and took a top edge on its way to Mooresy's gloves. Had he been standing any further back, it would have gone over his head for four. Robin Smith then joined Paul Terry and they mounted a recovery from four for two, Smith eventually falling to Sals for

124. By the end of the day they had reached 267 for nine. I was really pleased with the way Sals bowled. Our talk the other night, along with his hard work in the nets the day after, helped him to figures of four for 90 in 28 overs, including a wicket off the last ball of the day. Franklyn did even better with four for 41. The only criticism of our bowling is that Giddo and Jarv bowled too many loose balls, feeding Robin Smith in particular.

In conversation with Jarv at the end of the day, he expressed his disappointment at having bowled below par, and was annoyed at missing a very difficult chance to catch Benjamin at mid-off. He half expected to be jeered off the field, and I had to remind him that the Hove crowd is slightly more forgiving than Yorkshire folk. He was keen to impress today and perhaps tried a bit too hard.

13 May - Hampshire, second day

The second day against Hampshire started overcast, but the sun is threatening to appear. The wicket is likely to remain sporty and we'll have to be wary of Cowans and Benjamin. The start couldn't have been better. Franklyn runs up and Benjamin is caught behind off the first ball of the day. We then proceeded to collapse right from the word go. Billy Athey, Jamie Hall and Smithy shouldered arms to Cowans and were given out lbw without offering a shot. I unnecessarily chased a wide ball from Thursfield and was caught behind. Peter Moores played-on to James and as if in a blur we were 34 for five. Franklyn scored a whirlwind 25 but was out before lunch, leaving us on a hapless 73 for six. Martin

Speight and Sals batted brilliantly to rebuild the innings with a fabulous 126 from Speighty. The last three all added valuable runs, including an improbable 15 from Ed Giddins, to give us a slender lead of 12. We bowled 26 overs at them before the close and Franklyn had Terry caught behind. Our fight back today was stirring stuff. At 34 for five we were looking to survive, let alone take a lead! Sals was watched by Fred Titmus today and no doubt did his England chances no harm with good performances with bat and ball. He's certainly played his way back into the one-day side for Sunday.

Thinking about my own performance with the bat, the season's too short to throw away my wicket with loose and irresponsible shots, and I had plenty of time sitting in the pavilion today to sit back and reflect. It's interesting sitting in the dressing room when the top batsmen have been rolled over and are wondering what to do with themselves whilst someone else rescues the situation. Jamie Hall spent most of his day in a deck chair watching the game, Billy Athey sat in the viewing room reading the newspaper, watching TV and doing his crossword. I retired to the captain's room to seek solace and discuss with Giffy where it had all gone wrong. The top four were nowhere near positive enough.

We're in the process of moving house at the moment. With the pressure of desperately wanting to win something for Sussex, and throwing my wicket away twice, it difficult for me to think about anything other than cricket. The England squad for the one-day series is announced on Sunday. I don't expect to be selected but the ambition still eats away inside.

14 May - Hampshire, third day

Driving to the ground for day three against Hampshire, my mind was preoccupied with the significant improvement in Sals's bowling. He's now bowling a straight line which enables me to set a split field: square-leg, mid-wicket and mid-on; mid-off, extra cover and cover point. This allows the luxury of a slip, and a bat-pad on the off-side. A straight half-volley is harder to hit than a wide half-volley because a batsman can free his arms and attack the wide ball with a full swing of the bat. Forcing a batsman to work a straight ball to leg by playing across the line increases the chance of taking his wicket. When the ball is turning, it's possible to place another catcher near the bat, taken from mid-wicket, to encourage the batsman to play against the spin to work the mid-wicket gap. To a new batsman, bringing a man up on the sweep also increases the pressure by making it hard to get off the mark. Sals is now satisfied with this field, although it is very different to the one he had in the West Indies.

I'll be looking to control the game today by bowling tightly, setting defensive fields, and putting the Hampshire batsmen under pressure to score runs. The third innings is generally the hardest to bat in a championship game which is fairly equal, as it is difficult to create a winning platform and preserve wickets at the same time. The day started well enough: Jamie Hall took a blinding catch to dismiss Middleton; Morris was caught behind; Mark Nicholas was caught fending off a throat-ball; Robin Smith gloved an attempted pull to the keeper - all four wickets falling to Franklyn in an inspired spell giving him figures of 10 for 80 so far in the match, a first for him at Hove. Before lunch the rain set in and prevented any further play today.

15 May - Hampshire, Sunday League

A dreadful performance today in the Sunday League game. We won the toss and batted first, and although it was going to be difficult to score runs, there can be no excuses for a such a woeful effort, Keith Greenfield excepted, and we crashed to a second one-day defeat. We had to make three late changes to the team with Sals, John North and Carlos Remy coming into the side for the unfit Neil Lenham, David Smith and Eddie Hemmings. Billy Athey disappointed again, as did Martin Speight, who was stumped taking a wild swing at Maru. Speighty has to learn to curtail the rash elements in his game. There's no doubt he's a talented player, but you can't get by on flair alone. It must be harnessed to responsibility and application for his potential to be fully realised. My promising partnership with Keith Greenfield ended when I played around a full-toss from Udal, and we collapsed to a pathetic 161, with the added embarrassment of three amateurish run-outs.

For the first 10 overs they managed only 21 runs and we were still in the game, but the wheels came off again when Robin Smith and Paul Terry smacked the bowling to all parts. Sals was hit for 34 in only four overs and

Ed Giddins did just as badly. Giffy posed the question *"How many Sussex players have a burning desire to win?"* Losing really hurts, and I want all the players to know how it feels to congratulate the winning captain when your team has just been hammered. I'm in no way unsportsmanlike, but it's the pits and I'll never get used to it. I want to see more fight and responsibility from every one of the players, and I won't allow a situation to develop where the other counties see us as a team strong on paper but poor on the field. I don't want the players to be scared of losing, as this can inhibit a positive and winning approach. There's a real difference between trying to win and trying not to lose, and I know which I prefer. There's no such thing as 'just another day at the office' and 'we'll put it right tomorrow' sort of attitude as far as my cricket is concerned, and I want all the players to feel as passionately about winning as I do.

16 May - Hampshire, final day
What a difference a day makes, but why oh why do we contrive to make it so hard for ourselves. The day ended with a championship win, but with more a feeling of relief than elation. Franklyn took his sixth wicket of the innings, leaving him with 11 for 96 in the match. I switched Ed Giddins to the Cromwell Road end, and he charged in to take four wickets for five runs, including the last three in the space of four deliveries, leaving us 156 to win. Then the nightmare began.

We started off well enough, but were quickly three

down for 49. At tea we were 100 for four. I then nicked Benjamin to slip, having misjudged the line after going back and across my stumps. More disaster followed: we lost three wickets for one run and still needed nearly 50 to win with seven wickets down. Jarv and Peter Moores hit Benjamin for 29 runs in two overs, and I started to breathe more easily until Benjamin trapped Moores lbw in his next over. At this stage I certainly didn't fancy our chances of winning, but Eddie Hemmings and Jarv used their experience to guide us to a narrow victory. A post-mortem decided that, although we are a talented side, we are not yet a good one with all of us playing consistently enough to carry the team through difficult situations. We got away with it today and maybe it's a good sign.

At the wicket with Martin Speight today I tried to calm him down after he hoiked Cowans into the office for six. The next one was pitched up outside off-stump and he tries to swipe it over mid-on. Another word of caution from the captain. Next ball wide of off-stump, but full in length, and he plays-on trying to lash it through the covers! I need to talk to Speighty about his overwhelming desire to see the ball flying to the boundary with every shot. Opposing captains automatically set the field back for him and then wait for him to self-destruct. If he engaged his brain before he swings the bat, he would see that he can score a run a ball by knocking it around, and still hit boundaries by being more selective on what he spanks out of the ground.

Giddo bowled well today and received a well-earned pat on the back along with a reminder that we need this sort of performance every game, and against top order batsmen too. He has no less ability than Darren Gough, who has been selected for the England one-day side, but is as yet some way short of Gough's sheer hard work and consistency.

17 May

A day off today with my family. Time to spend on domestic issues with the house move imminent, and the added bonus of taking my mind off cricket for a few hours. I managed also to find time to visit my parents, and as ever with my father, the talk soon turned to cricket. His advice is to stop worrying about the possibility of selection for England, and to concentrate on enjoying my cricket. It's an important point and a good thought to return to when the pressure is on.

18 May

The routine for a travelling day is to report to the ground for training before setting off to the venue. Everyone has their own training routine, and today I did ten laps of the ground and some exercises with Peter Moores. Before lunch I sat down with Giffy to sort out the sides for the championship game and one-dayer at Notts. Before leaving for Trent Bridge there's a committee meeting to attend and I hope the cricketing matters on the agenda can be brought forward to allow us to get off early to Nottingham. The win against Hampshire will of course be slightly easier to explain than the loss it almost was. At committee meetings,

Giffy and myself report on the month's cricket for the first-team, second-eleven and all representative cricket in Sussex. The management of the club could not be more supportive in our quest for success. It is essential for a captain, and for the playing staff, to feel that they carry the support of the people who run the club. In my time as captain of Sussex I have never found that vital support to be lacking. When I was a young player, I felt far more remote from the management side of the club than young players do currently. There have been so many changes for the better in recent years, the club is much more professionally run and there is a tangible feeling of teamwork throughout the whole club.

19 May - Nottinghamshire at Trent Bridge, first day

On the injury front, going into today's game, Martin Speight has recovered from a groin strain (incurred trying to hit someone out of the ground no doubt), Smithy should be fit, but Neil Lenham's foot injury looks like preventing him from bowling for the rest of the season with a long lay-off in the winter to fully recover. Had a look at the wicket, which the groundsman admitted had been used by Notts for practice, as they want to play us on a used wicket. I'm not sure that's how the game should be played, but that's up to them.

I lost the toss, and not surprisingly Notts elected to bat. The first session seemed to have everything, Jamie Hall remarked that it was like the highlights from a days play compacted into one period. At lunch they were 130-odd for four. Jimmy Adams and Kevin Evans, who was dropped no less than three times, the third time by me when he was on 99, rattled along to a century apiece. They ended the day on 368 for seven. We bowled far too many loose deliveries and were hit for 54 boundaries in 110 overs.

20 May - Nottinghamshire, second day
Awoke to pouring rain and little prospect of play. It is possible that Notts will declare on 368 to keep the game alive. Alternatively, they could bat on and hope to bowl us out twice in two days. Losing a day to rain has not harmed our chances of winning the game, but due to the poor weather I've had only three proper championship innings and haven't really made a mark yet.

I managed to get through on the telephone to Steve Rhodes today to congratulate him on making the England side for the one-day games against New Zealand. I spent a lot of time with him in South Africa over the winter and feel sure that he can command a place in the side for years ahead.

21 May - Nottinghamshire, third day
We arrived at the ground only for the rain to start as soon as they took the covers off. By mid-afternoon it was still coming down heavily, and play was called off for the day. Now the negotiating will start to see if we can make a game of it on Monday. The wicket has definitely taken in some moisture and turned a bit green, and having spent two days in the changing room, there is no way I'll be happy chasing 300-plus. I

England A in South Africa.

The scoreboard at Wanderers shows five substitute fielders.

Press Day, and we show off our footwear.

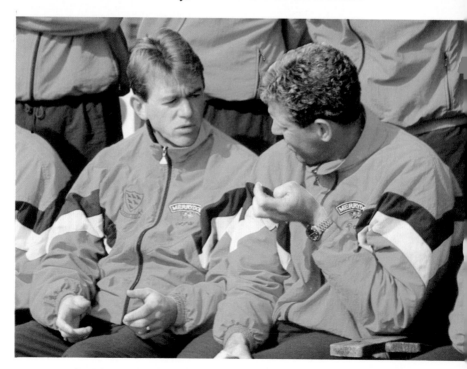

Grabbing an opportunity to discuss batting with David Smith.

A start of season interview with Tony Millard.

Peter Moores - when not playing he is invariably practising.

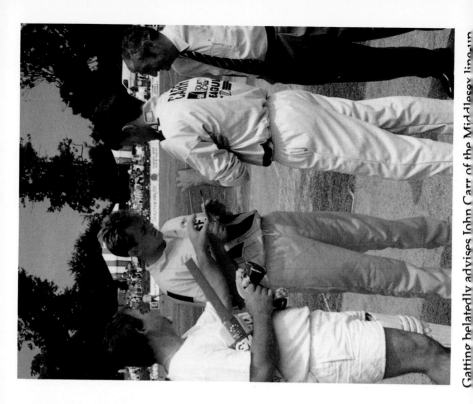

Franklyn Stephenson, who had an inspirational season.

Awarding a surprised Ed Giddins his county cap.

Two sides of captaincy.

Motivating players is a major part of captaincy.

A Sky interview before the Sunday game against Lancashire.

With two young Sussex supporters at Arundel.

Vith Kepler Wessels and Jim Parks before playing the touring South Africans.

Discussing the controversial line-up to face Derbyshire in the Sunday League.

learned my lesson on negotiated run-chases in my first season as captain, it may even have been my first game in charge. Mark Nicholas set us over 300 to win on the last day and even though we were an inexperienced side, I agreed to the chase and we never looked like coming close. A target discussed between captains on the last day always sounds tempting, but I'm more wary than I once was.

A day of inactivity is anathema to most cricketers, and we get as bored as the next person when cooped up in the pavilion all day watching the rain come down. Fortunately, there is a decent indoor school at Trent Bridge, so it was possible to have a net as a break from watching the TV and reading the newspapers. After that we dragged the nets back and sent Ed Giddins down to Tim Robinson's sports shop to buy a football for an impromptu game of four-a-side. The competitive spirit is never far away. A burst of physical activity at the end of a no-play day is essential to work off the extra food we all consume whilst sitting around doing nothing.

22 May - Nottinghamshire, Sunday League

One advantage of the new Sunday format is the opportunity it affords for a lie-in! Before the start of play, I wanted a discussion with all the team on our approach to and the fundamentals of one-day cricket. The weather made all our good intentions redundant, as it poured all day and we shared the points without taking the field.

Brian Bolus, the England selector, was at the ground

and he took me to one side with Norman Gifford to let me know that although my season hadn't started with a run-feast, there is no reason why I shouldn't remain in contention for a place. He has had good reports on me, particularly on the A Tour to South Africa, from Phil Neale, and it's a great relief to know that I am still under consideration. It's the first time a selector has spoken to me about playing for England, and I appreciated of being told where I stand. We work hard at Sussex to communicate with the players so they know exactly where they stand and what we expect from them. They can then concentrate on their game without the anxiety of uncertainty.

23 May - Nottinghamshire, final day

Tim Robinson offered me some declaration bowling first off to speed up the game and maximise his time bowling at us in the second innings. I was reluctant to agree to this, and settled for a short period of batting so that I could assess the wicket and not fall into the trap of being bowled out on a difficult wicket in our second innings. I wanted to chase 260-270 maximum, off 70 overs. Tim wanted more overs to bowl us out, so we settled on circa 280 in a minimum of 80 overs. In reality, we were faced with the prospect of scoring 288 in the second innings to win the game. We started brightly enough, the openers were still intact at lunch, and we were looking to score 100-110 in the 35 overs or so in the next session, with steady batting. This would leave us under 150 to get in the last session, which is feasible, providing there are wickets in hand.

Billy Athey and Jamie Hall batted brilliantly, and at tea we were well placed at 141 without loss. We'd back ourselves to score 147 runs in 35 overs, with 10 wickets remaining. With the score on 159, Jamie Hall was stumped dancing down the wicket on 56. Smithy was out for a duck. Jimmy Adams took the third wicket to fall within four overs when he bowled Billy Athey, six runs away from a deserved century.

The loss of quick wickets put the brakes on the chase, and in an effort to keep the tempo up I sent in Speighty ahead of me, on the basis that he is capable of hitting the spinners in a more unorthodox but effective way. He'll sweep anywhere between mid-wicket and very fine, and with his usual blend of cuts and reverse sweeps, I expected him to keep the scoreboard moving, which he did. We put on 40 runs together before Speighty was caught behind attempting to cut. I was joined by Carlos Remy batting at six. As good a player as Carlos is, a lack of experience in a pressure situation was his downfall. He has bags of talent but was noticeably nervous when he came to the crease. Watching Carlos trying to get off the mark built up pressure on me as the overs slipped away. Instead of pushing it around into the gaps I had to go for boundaries, and was out for 44 to a shot I wouldn't normally play. We still needed 39 in about seven overs. Peter Moores and Carlos Remy took the score along to 277 for five, then four wickets fell inside two overs for just one run, and we fell short of winning the game by 10 runs. Eddie Hemmings came to the rescue for the second championship match in succession, and defied his old county by blocking the last few balls to give us a draw. We felt as if we had lost the game after reaching such a strong position, and the dressing room was like a morgue. With so many rain-affected games, we missed a great opportunity to close in on the leaders, with the advantage of a game in hand.

24 May

Practice at the ground today and there is still a lot of tension around following the draw yesterday. It was obvious that the players are still smarting, and in many ways it's a positive sign, as the pain in defeat which was lacking earlier will strengthen their resolve for the games to come.

25 May

The feeling of disappointment has gone and the guys are raring to go against Glamorgan tomorrow. We're constantly in touch with Chris Waller, the second-team coach, about how the players are performing, which is not only vital for selection purposes but for all the first-team to keep in touch with results for Sussex as a whole. Although we have separate schedules and matches, we all play for the same county and I want the second-team players to realise that they are only one step away from first-team cricket.

26 May - Glamorgan at Hove, first day

Yet another cold, wet and miserable day with no prospect of play. Matthew Maynard is out of the Glamorgan side with a broken knuckle, but in any case we fancy our chances for a win, although three days play only reduces the chance of a result. The only team change will be to bring back Ed Giddins for Carlos Remy, as we need the services of a third seamer on this wicket. Neil Lenham is fit again, to bat, but I'd like to try him in a one-day game before bringing him back into the championship side. In any event, Jamie Hall deserves to keep his place and there's no justification for him to make way for a returning Lenham.

27 May - Glamorgan, second day

At last the rain has stopped but it is still overcast. The ground is very quick-drying so we shouldn't miss more than a session. The day started with Eddie Hemmings telling me that his calf is still a problem, and as much as he wants to play, his experience tells him that it's more responsible to make way for a fit player rather than let the side down by failing to perform because of an injury. Keith Greenfield will come in to replace Eddie. Ideally, I would like to put them in, declare our first innings, and end up with a run-chase on the final day to win the game. The first part of the plan worked, but instead of dismissing them, they scored almost 400, with centuries from Adrian Dale and Hugh Morris. The first session was one of playing and missing, interspersed with boundaries. Prior to lunch we missed a chance to run-out Hugh Morris. Jamie Hall sent in a superb throw from the deep to Sals, who was hovering over the stumps, whilst the batsmen held a mid-wicket conference to decide which end they were going to run to. The ball landed safely in Sals' hands but unluckily he trod on the stumps before he could break the wicket with the ball! We desperately wanted a good start as Glamorgan have started poorly this season. Ed Giddins bowled well down the hill after lunch, but without Hemmings I couldn't find a partner for him to tie-up the other end.

28 May - Glamorgan, third day

Glamorgan batted on to declare at 432 for six and we failed to take the seventh wicket and earn an extra bowling point. Jamie Hall and Billy Athey got us off to a good start and I went to the crease to join Smithy at 87 for two. Time was running out in the game, the field was defensive, so we decided to hit out. I only made 24, but for the first time this year I can say that I was a touch unlucky in getting out. The ball kept low, hit the underneath of the bat and was caught by Colin Metson standing up to Adrian Dale. Smithy carried on the fight and scored 74. I reviewed the position at tea, and was looking for 250 by batting steadily, and then launching an assault to reach 300 as quickly as possible, to give us time to bowl this evening. Peter Moores hit an excellent 70, well supported by Keith Greenfield with 34. Hugh Morris played his part in keeping the game alive by setting attacking fields when it became clear that he wasn't going to bowl us out before the follow-on target. We declared at 300, and with a full-house of lights on the scoreboard, Billy Athey and myself opened the bowling to keep us on the field. However, I don't expect an easy target for Monday.

My son Luke is away this weekend with my sister-in-law. Melanie enjoyed the break and joined us at the club for a drink before we went out together for the evening. We were able to discuss my feelings regarding my ambitions for the season, and basically she advised me to stop feeling sorry for myself, cut out the worrying and concentrate on playing the way I've always played. Of course, she's absolutely right.

29 May - Glamorgan, Sunday League

Seemingly cricket weather at last. I have the unenviable task of telling Billy Athey that his role as opening batsman, responsible for moving the score along early in a one-day innings, is just not working, and he'll be left out of the team today. We'll open with Keith Greenfield and David Smith. Sals will also be left out as his confidence is still brittle, and if a batsman gets after him, his control tends to desert him. Leaving him out of the side may not sound like the obvious way of rebuilding his confidence, but we need him to perform in championship games, and I won't risk that by throwing him to the lions in one-day slogs.

Before the start I took Franklyn and Jarv to the wicket and against my better judgement they talked me into batting first. Fortunately, the decision was taken out of my hands when Hugh Morris won the toss and elected to bat. We actually played to our potential today, restricting Glamorgan to 139 in 40 overs through tight bowling and sharp fielding. After a couple of stoppages due to rain, our reduced target was 115 in 33 overs, which we made with overs to spare.

30 May - Glamorgan, final day

The sun is out and I'm looking forward to a run-chase today. I feel positive and fancy scoring a few runs. Normally I'd keep such wild and confident thoughts to myself, as the best way to be out for a duck is to tell your fellow professionals how good you feel just before you walk to the wicket! With our strong batting line up, Peter Moores at seven and Franklyn at eight, anything is possible.

I hate having to send down joke bowling, and thankfully it wasn't required in order for Hugh to declare and set us 320 to win in 75 overs. Ed Giddins bowled exceptionally well, taking three for 45 in 12 attacking overs. He is really bending his back at the moment and I feel we are at last getting the best out of him. We started the chase badly by losing two wickets for 18 runs, then Jamie Hall and myself enjoyed a partnership of 130. I was next out for 64 and felt really bad as I had carefully laid the foundation to play a big innings and win the game. Bastien was bowling and I made the mistake of deciding before the ball was bowled to drop it at my feet and take a quick single. Inevitably, the ball was wider than I anticipated and I nicked it to the keeper. Speighty was out next ball, and my intent then was to abandon the chase and settle for a draw. Franklyn's idea of blocking is obviously a little different to mine. Before he went in to bat, I asked him just to hang around until the end of play. He reached the crease with one hour and 20 overs to go, and only four wickets left. He whacked his first ball over the head of mid-wicket for four, and proceeded to blaze away like a lunatic, ending up with 71 not out. So much for my instruction to him to just bat for an hour! We ended up 60 runs light and the game ended in a draw.

1 June
Practice today and a long session with Giffy to pick the team to play Kent. Sals is doubtful because of a shoulder injury. Neil Lenham is fit again and scoring runs for the seconds, but it would be wrong for me to drop Jamie Hall to accommodate him.

2 June - Kent at Tunbridge Wells, first day
I always look forward to playing at Tunbridge Wells. It's normally a result wicket, with spongy bounce and a tendency to swing. Kent have lost three out of four and we are looking to turn that into four out of five. My hope for this match is good performances throughout the team, especially in the batting. So far we've lacked consistency, and although a bowler or batsman has shined individually, we haven't really clicked as a team yet. I had earlier made up my mind to put Kent in if I won the toss, but as the coin was in the air I changed my mind and decided we would bat, much to the surprise of the senior players looking on. Billy Athey and Jamie Hall put on 118 and by the end of play we would have been struggling without Billy's eventual 166 not out, which took us to 305 for seven. The consistency I was hoping for failed to materialise, and once again I was out after getting a start - that is if you ignore being dropped on nought by Carl Hooper. To give them credit, the Kent bowlers recovered well

after tea and deserved their wickets.

Playing on my mind at the moment is the fact that my highest score so far this season is only 64. I'm trying to prevent any anxiety coming with me to the crease, as I know how hard it is to score runs when you place yourself under enormous pressure every time you walk to the wicket.

3 June - Kent, second day

Today we need to add 50 or so to our overnight score, as scoring in later innings will not be easy on a wicket which is slowing and beginning to turn. With Lancashire next at Horsham, a venue at which we usually do well, we need to beat Kent to maintain the momentum.

Having added only 14 runs to our first innings total the weather conditions really hampered us today, even though it remained dry. There was a gale-force wind blowing most of the day and the seamers found it hard going, despite a terrific spell from Jarv, who bowled for almost a complete session. In Giddo's first over I moved gulley to give him some protection, and lo and behold, the next ball took off and Mark Benson fended it off to exactly where I had had a fielder the ball before. Naturally, the players didn't fail to notice such an inspired piece of captaincy. Such is the joy of being in charge. Eddie Hemmings ended up shouldering most of the burden, bowling 30 overs into the wind, and even took his second diving catch of the season. We stuck at it, but Kent ended up fairly well placed on 336 for six, with good contributions from nearly all the batsmen.

Speighty was hit on the hand fielding close to the bat when Trevor Ward pulled a short ball from Hemmings. He went to hospital where an X-ray confirmed nothing broken. It does, however, look as if he will find it difficult to bat in our second innings, and adds to my selection problems for the Sunday game. We found the energy to stop for a drink on the way home, and seeing the guys slumped in armchairs made me realise how much effort they had put in today.

4 June - Kent, third day
The day started cloudy with rain, no play being possible, and by mid-afternoon I was driving home. A miserable day in every respect. If we are to make a game of it a contrived finish will be necessary on Monday, and I'll have to come to some agreement with Mark Benson.

5 June - Kent, Sunday League
I played John North today in place of Speighty. We batted first, posted 208, and Kent comfortably passed our score with over two overs to spare. Smithy pulled a muscle in his groin during his innings, whilst I concentrated on anchoring one end to enable the others to keep the score going. It wasn't my natural game and I need to consider whether it's a sensible tactic.

Looking ahead to tomorrow, providing play is possible, Mark Benson has two choices. To bat on, take a reasonable lead and hope to bowl us out to win the game. Or to sit down and negotiate a run-chase, which would be very embarrassing as he would have to send down 21 overs of rubbish to set it up. That would be dreadful and I can't imagine anything worse.

6 June - Kent, final day

Mark Benson declared at the overnight score of 336 for six, taking a slender lead of 17. He did not want to send down joke bowling from the start in order to set up a last innings chase for Kent, as he fancied his chances of bowling us out and knocking off not too many runs to win the match. Always a tough negotiator, Benson wanted it both ways and asked me to agree to giving him two chances to win: to try for 90 minutes or so to bowl us out, then failing that to send down some rubbish for us to slog and set them a target. I certainly wasn't going to give him two bites of the cherry, so our second innings commenced with the Kent bowlers hoping to bowl us out cheaply.

We still made hard work of it and slumped to 15 for two, then into further trouble at 155 for six. Martin Speight may be a flamboyant strokemaker but he also has courage and grit. After sustaining a nasty blow on the second day, he came in at eight to bat for over an hour, for only 18 runs, in a 50-plus partnership with Peter Moores which held the innings together. It was a day for brave efforts as earlier on Smithy had fought his way to a half-century, employing Jamie Hall as a runner.

I was determined not to let the game fizzle out in a tame draw, and mindful of the fact that spectators pay good money to see a game of cricket, I declared, leaving Kent a victory target of 221 in 25 overs. They are an attacking side, and they opened with Ward and Fleming, the Sunday League partnership. Both batsmen went for their shots from the very first over. At one stage I had fielders all around the boundary to keep the runs down. A Kent supporter in the crowd shouted out *"I suppose you'll have the keeper on the boundary soon."* I replied by saying that if we conceded a few byes then I might just do that. He should have been grateful that he was being entertained. It's rare for me to actually notice what is being said by someone in the crowd, even though with some of the lamentable attendances at county games you'd think you would hear someone whispering in the pavilion. In the middle, concentrating on the game, you just don't hear it.

Most captains in my position wouldn't even contemplate the possibility of declaring and taking 10 wickets in 25 overs, let alone give the opposition a sniff of victory. With 79 needed from the last eight overs, and eight wickets in hand, I felt a flash of panic before Franklyn took two quick wickets and they shut up shop. Marsh came out to bat, and although I tried to encourage him by bringing on Billy Athey for an over of off-spin, with close fielders, he wasn't interested and we called it a day.

9 June - Lancashire at Horsham, first day
Horsham is a ground on which you hope to win the toss. The wicket suits our bowling and batting. It offers bounce and turn for the bowlers and short boundaries with the ball coming onto the bat for the batsmen. I won the toss and was looking for the classic four-day

scenario: bat first, post a large total, and bowl them out twice. Only Neil Lenham was out cheaply, but despite the rest of the batsmen getting a start, we all failed to go on and make a telling score, with the exception of Jamie Hall who battled well for his third half-century of the season. I made 34 and never felt comfortable within myself. At this stage of the season I normally have a couple of good scores under my belt, but runs are elusive at the moment.

Not for the first time this season, Franklyn rescued the situation with a fine batting display, leaving him eight runs short of his century at the close of play. His innings was a controlled mix of explosive hitting and sensible defence. Jarv proved his worth with the bat by contributing a useful 44. Looking on, seeing them progress at four an over, I felt that their partnership was going to be significant, and perhaps determine the course of the game. Our middle order has been inconsistent, bordering on the fragile, and an indication of a good team performance is the ability of the lower order to make telling contributions when needed.

10 June - Lancashire at Horsham, second day
We added only 22 to our overnight score, falling some way short of the 400 I hoped we would reach on what is essentially a batting wicket. At least Franklyn reached his century. Lancashire are an extremely strong and talented batting side. They bat all the way down: every player in their side has scored a first-class hundred, and consequently there is no tail. It will be hard work to take 10 genuine wickets.

We couldn't have had a better start, with Franklyn having the England captain caught behind for a duck. Gallian, a threatening and emerging batsman, and Crawley, whose prodigious talent I witnessed first-hand in South Africa, both got a start but were out relatively cheaply. Giddo had the dangerous Fairbrother caught by Sals, also for a duck, and at 82 for four they were wobbling. Nick Speak breathed some life back into their innings, then I recalled Giddo for what proved to be a devastating spell.

When Giddo puts his heart and soul into his bowling and slots into his rhythm, he can be as lethal as anyone else on the circuit. He steamed in to take four wickets in 14 balls, for only four runs. He ended Speak's resistance with a yorker, did the same to Graham Lloyd, bowled Akram for a duck, then accounted for Hegg leg-before. When he bowls, he presents the seam better than any bowler in the side, and when he hits the spot consistently, anything can happen. At 154 for eight, I was weighing up our options, as they were still 52 runs short of the follow-on. I expected the wicket to wear and asked the senior players what they thought of the idea of us batting again, rather than enforcing the follow-on. In the end, the decision was taken out of my hands as Mike Watkinson and Peter Martin enjoyed a last-wicket partnership of 93 to reduce the deficit to under 100.

11 June - Lancashire at Horsham, third day
Not for the first time I reminded the players that the third innings is often the hardest. I wanted

concentration and application from all the batsmen, as we had to score sufficient runs to put the game beyond Lancashire's reach. Atherton, Akram and Fairbrother would not all be out for zero a second time.

Akram is a feared bowler. He can be devastating, and can run through a side before you know what's happened. On this occasion, although his opening burst was fiery, he seemed to lack interest. We batted steadily and Neil Lenham top-scored with an excellent century. I made 61, an improvement on my first innings effort, but again I never really felt in control. I should have gone on to a big innings, but although I was physically at the crease, my mind was elsewhere. I needed to balance the declaration by giving us enough time to bowl them out, and eventually closed our innings leaving Lancashire to score over 450 to win.

12 June - Lancashire at Horsham, Sunday League
We crashed to a second successive Sunday League defeat by failing to score anywhere near enough runs after batting first. The start was reasonable enough, but the last five wickets yielded a paltry 26 runs, with three going in the final over. We never looked like bowling them out and Mike Atherton notched up a handsome century, ably supported by Gallian, to win the match with seven wickets to spare.

13 June - Lancashire at Horsham, final day
The final day provided a classic finish to a four-day game. The wicket was offering turn, so the spinners had to do most of the work. Sals took the prize wickets of

Atherton and Crawley in the morning session, but we struggled to make inroads after lunch, thanks to solid batting from Speak and Lloyd. John Crawley caught me in the first innings and I was delighted to return the compliment in Lancashire's second. I was beginning to think that if they kept going, a platform could be established for on onslaught in the last 30 overs. Even when they were six down, with less than 25 overs to bowl, we still had a lot to do to take the last four wickets. Akram strolled to the crease and proceeded to hit out as only he can. The ball was flying to the boundary with seemingly alarming regularity, but inside I was pleased that he was playing big shots to almost every ball. On a turning wicket, against two class spinners, Akram was going to get himself out. Although there was a short boundary, and he was striking the ball as cleanly as I have ever seen it struck, it didn't take a lot of bravery to keep Hemmings and Sals on, as I knew that there would be only one winner. At nine wickets down, Akram was still going for it and he was finally yorked by Eddie Hemmings, two runs short of a century. The spinners took eight wickets between them, with Sals bowling exceptionally well for his first five-wicket haul since the end of last season. A classic contest ended with our second championship win this year.

I was surprised that Lancashire kept going in the way they did. A draw was perhaps the most likely outcome, yet they seemed determined to go for an outrageous win, or perish in the attempt. I considered that at this stage of the season they did not see us as a threat, and were prepared to risk giving us the points for a win, rather than deny us by playing for a draw. Because of the huge points differential between a draw and a win, the championship is always more tactical than it looks to the outside eye. You have to continually assess how a result will effect your own position, and that of your opponents too. The difference between a draw and a defeat is little in points, but no captain wants to gift winning points to the opposition when they might pay for it later in the season.

16 June - Durham at Hove, first day

Not a cloud in the sky and a wicket which is ". . . *as dry as the Sahara"*, according to the groundsman. Let's hope it's more bouncy! Smithy is fit again but I can't find space for him in the side with Jamie Hall and Neil Lenham playing so well. Smithy understands and accepts the situation, the experienced pro that he is. I'm looking forward to continuing where we left off against Lancashire, although Durham are buzzing at the moment and will be hard to beat.

At one stage it looked as if we would be facing a huge Durham first innings total, after they won the toss and batted first. By lunch they were 138 for one off 39 overs, and I was wondering how we were going to stop them scoring and take the remaining nine wickets. Larkins and Saxelby were in full flow and made 78 and 50 respectively. John Morris hit 28, typically all in boundaries. His style is to wait for the loose ball then give it the full treatment. Durham are full of shot-makers and it's a matter of the bowler's patience outlasting the batsman's. The bowlers have to avoid too much experimentation in an attempt to force wickets. If the ball doesn't seam, then bowlers like Jarv and Giddo will try and swing it. If it fails to swing, then it's a matter of relying on line and length, and pressurising the batsmen to take liberties against Sals or Eddie Hemmings at the other end.

The waiting game started to pay off and we took five wickets for about 100 runs, leaving Durham five down at tea. After Giddo had Larkins caught behind, I brought on Jarv to bowl at the new batsman. Reflecting on this later in the afternoon, I realised that I should have had the spinners working in harness, but I didn't, and allowed Scott and Cummins to stage a mini-recovery. Giddo replaced a tired Sals at the sea end but came off after one over. Eddie Hemmings was frustrated at not being able to bowl from the end Sals had taken his wickets from. For 10 minutes or so they were both bending my ear on the field, so I bowled Billy Athey for one over to facilitate a change of ends for the two complaining bowlers. To my amazement, Cummins tried to pull a ball from Billy and he scooped it down to long leg where Franklyn Stephenson took a comfortable catch. Another piece of inspired captaincy! After tea we cleaned up the remaining wickets and they finished on 278 all out.

Jamie Hall and Billy Athey rounded off a good day by putting on 54 runs without loss, and we'll be looking to consolidate tomorrow and posting a match-winning first innings total. The Durham bowling attack is not the most feared on the circuit: Cummins is the main strike bowler and is certainly quick; Brown offers a little variety with left-arm over; Wood and Walker are similar bowlers; and Graveney is the only spinner.

17 June - Durham, second day

Today went well for us. We finished on 411 to take a lead of 133. Billy Athey was the only player to make over 50 and he did so in style with a brilliant 166. I made 48, Martin Speight 49, and most of the other players chipped in with something. As with Durham in their first innings, at one stage we looked like scoring in excess of 500, but their seam bowlers stuck at it and Cummins took five wickets - they took our last six wickets for less than 100 runs.

I am still frustrated with my own form - having made 48, the foundation was there to make a big score. The hard work had been done, although I struggled for rhythm and my footwork was leaden. After lunch I tried to hook Cummins and succeeded only in giving the keeper a catch off a top edge. The ball sat up, was asking to be hit, I could so easily have swayed out of the way, but at the time all I thought of was that it's one of my shots, and with a half-century beckoning, I played it. I always like to extract something positive out of a situation which has gone wrong, and today I overcame the initial insecurity of poor form by telling myself to be patient, keep working and occupy the crease.

Thoughts on one-day cricket team selection occupied my mind after play. Since we left Billy Athey out of the Sunday side, he has scored two big hundreds and I might do a direct swap for Keith Greenfield, whose bowling is not considered good enough at the moment to fill the sixth bowling slot, whereas Athey's can be. If we play Sals and Eddie Hemmings anyway, then having another spinner as the sixth bowler is a luxury I can do without. Another worry at the moment is what to do with David Smith. He was playing well before becoming injured, in championship games and one-day matches. With the Nat West game looming next week I need to find room for him in the side, but at whose expense, as the other batsmen have done well recently. Jamie Hall is a likely candidate but this would be really hard on him, because when he came into the one-day side last Sunday against Lancashire, he seized his chance and scored 69. Given that Smithy's last Nat West innings was in last year's final, when he scored a glorious century, I'll need to think long and hard before making my mind up on who should play.

After a satisfactory day's cricket, I had the added pleasure of driving in a different direction to our new home, as today we moved house.

18 June - Durham, third day

The third, and what turned out to be the final day's play in the four-day championship match against Durham. We bowled them out for 241, which left us with 108 to win. Eddie Hemmings was in vintage form and took five for 53. We polished off the runs for the loss of two wickets, and I managed to reach the right side of 50 by playing my natural game and taking the game to the bowlers.

There is a new attitude in the team at the moment. The confidence is high and they feel like winners. The talk over a beer in the squash club after the game was all about the form of the sides above us in the championship table, and who has how many points. Of the five sides ahead on points, four are not in winning positions, so we could well move up the table. It's genuinely exciting to witness the guys discussing the prospects for the matches to come, and to see a controlled confidence growing in the team. The players are starting to believe in each other and I have always felt that confidence would be generated if our collective ability is realised on the field.

The way Sals is bowling is one of the keys to our success at the moment. He really is bowling as well as he ever has done. The wicket in this game was by no means a *bunsen-burner*, but Sals' good form has made things happen. Eddie Hemmings is just Eddie Hemmings - accurate, professional and forever thinking about how to get the batsman out. A feature of championship-winning sides is the ability of their players to step in with significant contributions at crucial stages, when the leading protagonists have failed. What I am finding satisfying about our championship performances so far is that we have also managed this - witness Franklyn and Jarv's partnership at Horsham against Lancashire. No one individual has set the game alight, but everyone is making telling contributions when it really matters. A balanced combination of individual feats and collective team effort wins championships, and this is what I'm striving for in this Sussex side.

19 June - Durham, Sunday League

I find it hard to see how I could make any changes to the side at the moment, so I started the day prepared to disappoint Smithy and Keith Greenfield. After lengthy team selection discussions, I decided to keep faith with Jamie Hall and Keith Greenfield as the opening batsmen. I then sat down with Billy Athey to explain that the current openers had got us off to good starts in recent matches, and there wasn't a place for him in today's team. In Wayne Larkins and John Morris Durham have a couple of seasoned and dangerous one-day batsmen, and Johnny Longley, the young lad who has moved from Kent, is a useful batsman and a good runner between the wickets. After a dismal start to our Sunday programme, we desperately needed a win, but we crashed to yet another defeat.

Our batting failed miserably. Whenever we looked like building a partnership someone got themselves out. Franklyn ran out Neil Lenham, then was caught trying to hit over mid-off. To see him sitting in the dressing room with his head in his hands for half an hour meant that he didn't need me to tell him what he'd done wrong.

I learned a lot from today in terms of team selection. No matter how well Keith Greenfield and Jamie Hall play, I am deluding myself by thinking that at this stage they have the experience of David Smith or Billy Athey to bat through an innings. As talented as they are, I have to realise that at times there is no substitute for experience. There is no doubt that they have the ability, but the know-how is still lacking, and it couldn't have been more evident today. They got us off to another good start, and then just as they looked set, got out. I'll have to return to Smithy and Athey for the forthcoming Nat West game against Essex. There is also an element of not exposing young players to too many situations beyond their experience, as their growing confidence could easily be eroded.

21 June - Essex at Hove, Nat West

A big game today against Essex in the first round of the Nat West. I've decided that we'll play the main five bowlers, with Billy Athey as the sixth. In a 60-over match you need the comfort of a back-up bowler because if one of the first five is off form, and being carted around the ground, 12 overs is a lot to get through. I won the toss and put Essex in to bat. I was hopeful of quick wickets on a pitch with a green tinge after a rain-delayed start. Gooch and Stephenson raced away and I was forced almost immediately into setting defensive fields, with sweepers on both sides of the wicket. To try and constrain Gooch, I used a tactic I'd deployed against Hampshire last year when Robin Smith was batting - setting the field back and attempting to keep him away from the strike. I had a feeling that Gooch was saving himself for an onslaught on the last nine overs of spin from Sals and Hemmings. Although we managed to put a break on his scoring, he still made 86. I felt fortunate that we restricted the total to 272, as it could easily have been in excess of 300.

The Essex bowling is not what it was. With the retirement of Pringle and Foster they have lost the experience of bowling at the death, and we have every chance of winning the match when we bat tomorrow.

22 June - Essex, Nat West

Two things to say to the team this morning before we bat. Essex scored 50 off the first 10 overs, then 222 off the next 50. We need to reverse that and aim to make 223 off the first 50, only a fraction above four an over, to leave us with 50 runs to score off the last 10 overs. Taken in the context of a championship game, would Essex declare to leave us a winning target of 273 in 60 overs, with a bowling attack limited to a maximum of 12 overs each?

The day started brightly enough with an opening stand of 40 from Smithy and Billy Athey. After the first wicket fell it was all downhill and the dream turned into a nightmare. Smithy pulled a groin muscle and retired hurt. I came in to join Speighty and played if not the most irresponsible shot of my career, then certainly the worst since I became captain of Sussex. I tried to play a reverse sweep off Pearson, the young off-spinner. The ball was wide down the leg side and instead of sweeping it fine I dragged it square and was caught. Walking off the field I could feel the whole crowd looking at me and thinking what a stupid shot it was to attempt at this stage. The stony silence from the pavilion left me in no doubt that it was a pathetic shot. At lunch a member approached me and said *"Wells, that reverse sweep was suicide."* Despite the fact that we are so accessible to the crowd, in all my years of playing I can't recall an incidence of a spectator coming up to me during a game and actually berating me for playing a bad shot. In reply, to illustrate the sometimes wafer-thin line between success and failure when batting, I said that had the ball sped to the boundary he would have been applauding rather than criticising. I wanted to highlight the fact that frequently in cricket an untypical error of judgement, or the thickness of the edge of the bat, can be the difference between being the hero or villain. I didn't need reminding of the villainous implications of the reverse sweep, and was well aware that there was no excuse for letting down the team, and the Sussex faithful. The shot itself is one I normally play with relative impunity, but deciding when to play it is as important as how it is played, and in this case there couldn't have been a worse time.

In the space of three overs, Speighty was run-out by an inspired piece of fielding by Hussain, and Franklyn was bowled attempting a third booming back foot drive. Neil Lenham stayed in whilst the carnage continued at the other end, and he was supported by a heroic performance from Smithy who returned with a runner to hit a typically pugnacious 64 before getting out with 94 needed from the last 10 overs. Neil Lenham continued to hit out but simply ran out of partners. He and Ed Giddins took the game into the last over with a last wicket stand of 35 runs off as many balls. Forced into a situation where they had to run for everything Giddo was run-out in the last over, and the valiant

Lenham was left stranded on a brave 82.

We may as well have lost by 160 runs, and the fact that after self-destructing we almost got out of jail, makes the loss doubly infuriating. The presentations after the match highlighted the contrast between last year and this. I sat there feeling incredibly low and could not stop my mind replaying the dreadful shot I had played at such a crucial time in the match. I gazed out blankly at Peter Eaton tending the square, going through his tasks as he does at the end of every game. Watching him made me realise that there are others at the club who feel a similar sense of disappointment, but just get on with the job in hand. It takes a while to accept that the deed has been done, and to realise that I'm not going to suddenly find myself at the crease having had a bad dream on the way to the wicket. The highs and lows in cricket never cease to amaze me. Sitting there, listening to the man of the match presentation to Essex's Ronnie Irani, I felt like picking up the microphone and apologising to the Sussex supporters for both my own individual transgression and the failure of the team to win the match - I felt so responsible for the defeat. I'm experienced enough to distinguish between the feelings of self pity which can accompany disappointment, and genuine regret when something has not gone as well as you would have liked, and the supporters had hoped. Thankfully, cricket is still a game where the players are close to the supporters, and it really hurt to see the disappointment on their faces.

This season, in contrast to last year, I've singularly

failed to carry the team to a one-day victory with my batting - it's a bitter pill to swallow. One of the most challenging, and also frustrating elements of batting is the ability of the mind to analyse and play flashbacks of every poor shot you've ever played. To turn it round to replay match-winning innings takes a deliberate and structured mental approach, so hard to recreate when your mind is flooded with negative thoughts. Captaining a side presents further challenges. To get the best out of the team, your own mind and motivation must be strong, and after every setback I can still find consolation in the realisation that in cricket you never stop learning, and there are always new barriers to be overcome. How ironic that the first boundary we hit in the semi-final last year was when I reverse swept Croft for four. I'll never play the reverse sweep again so early in an innings.

So at this stage of the season we are out of the B & H, out of the Nat West and making no impact in the Sunday League. Tomorrow is another day and I'll be ready to pick the team up for the championship matches to come.

23 June - Worcestershire at New Road, first day
Waking up this morning, the bad memories of yesterday are starting to diminish, especially after a few glasses of wine last night with Sals and Peter Moores. Picking up the newspapers to *"Reverse sweep sets Sussex on the path to defeat"* headlines on the sports pages soon brings me back to reality. The reports are scathing and I can't argue with them.

I was very pleased with the mood in the dressing room before play. After the misery of yesterday I really wanted to dispel the gloom, and strangely enough, no one was short of advice on how to play the reverse sweep! We enjoyed a funny five minutes in the nets, when everyone decided there was an urgent need to practice and perfect the shot. On the subject of unorthodox shots, we are all waiting for Speighty to invent a new stroke. I feel he is the ideal batsman to perfect the reverse hook or something equally outrageous. I recalled the lighter side of playing the reverse sweep, against Scotland in our first game of the season. The spinner must have spotted me changing my grip and he fired the ball down the leg side, leaving me looking like a complete idiot in position for the reverse sweep, letting the ball go through to the keeper. Smithy, an orthodox batsman if ever I saw one, was doubled up in laughter at the other end.

We've bought a party of 13 to Worcester for our eighth championship match of the season. Nicky Phillips is here to cover for Eddie Hemmings, who has a slight groin strain, and Carlos Remy is cover if we need a fourth seamer. I had a word with the Essex guys who played at New Road last and they said the wicket failed to offer any turn, and from back off a length the ball was as likely to scuttle along the ground as it was to fly past your nose. A late decision is therefore required on whether to risk Eddie Hemmings or go for a fourth seamer.

Hot and humid today and after Eddie Hemmings declared himself fit, I decided to bat first. The ball swung around in the early stages and we made 295. I was out for four to Tom Moody, a genuine dismissal to a ball that bounced up and took the top inside edge of my bat to loop up for an easy catch at bat-pad. Martin Speight didn't look comfortable at all and seems to be lacking in confidence at the moment. He may need a short spell in the second-team, with Keith Greenfield knocking at the door. Peter Moores and Neil Lenham steadied the ship then Franklyn opened his shoulders to score 95. Ed Giddins walked to the wicket with five runs needed for a batting bonus point and for a well-deserved century for Franklyn. This was a signal for Franklyn to kill two birds with one stone, and he perished trying to slog the ball out the ground.

This season we've often bowled too many loose deliveries at the start of an innings in an attempt to force wickets. I instructed the bowlers to keep to a disciplined line and length, and to resist the temptation to experiment. Unfortunately, this plea fell on deaf ears in Jarv's case and he was hit for 28 in three overs. Ed Giddins repaired the damage by taking the vital wickets of Curtis and Hick. It's always a relief to take Hick's wicket: he edged a ball wide of off stump which bounced and left him, Sals taking a good catch at slip. Eddie Hemmings bowled his normal steady spell into the wind. Sals bowled two beauties to Tom Moody in the last over of the day, and I think the spinners will play a major role on this wicket tomorrow. Overnight they were 73 for two.

24 June - Worcestershire, second day

Sals opened the bowling, and the day was dominated by the spinners, who exercised outstanding control on a turning wicket. Tom Moody was the first to fall, caught and bowled by Sals, who ended the day with five for 79. Eddie Hemmings chipped in with three for 70. We looked poised to take a first innings lead but the initiative was lost when Worcestershire added almost 100 runs for the last three wickets. When Sals bowls as well as this, my only concern, although concern isn't quite the right word, is that we will probably lose him to Test cricket. We reached 42 for one, with Jamie Hall the victim of a dubious decision, given out caught at slip off his pad. Although batting will still be difficult tomorrow, despite the short boundary on one side, I'd back us to defend 250 on this wicket.

25 June - Worcestershire, third day

Neil Lenham was out third ball this morning, and due to some tight bowling it was hard for us to move the score along. Billy Athey was out just after lunch for a gritty 57. Speighty rode his luck to score a typically adventurous 81, after I'd fallen for 38. Speighty's innings illustrated how difficult it is to leave him out the side, as he is always likely to produce something special. We ended up with a lead of 236, and the key session for us was between lunch and tea when we lost six wickets. Five of us were victims of our own mistakes, and the failure of the middle order, myself included, is regrettably becoming a feature of our batting this season.

Franklyn and Jarv opened the bowling and once again the opposition scored 30 or 40 runs in no time at all. Franklyn trapped Curtis lbw, and shortly afterwards I dropped Hick at first slip before he had scored. Hick is not a person to miss on nought in any game, in any situation, and I felt dreadful to drop him in such a tight match. After such a big miss your head drops for a while before you recover your composure and feel that you are back in the game. As an ordinary fielder, there's often a bit of space and time to recover your concentration, but as captain it's vital to dismiss the aberration from your mind instantly, and this is easier said than done with bowling changes and field placings to think of. I could see the anguish on the faces of the rest of the team: they knew as well as I did that it was likely to be a turning point, and the buzz with which we started the innings evaporated. They still need 170 which is a lot to get on this wicket.

Looking ahead to the Sunday game, it might be time to take the bull by the horns. I'm considering asking Speighty to open the batting, with a licence to smack the bowling to all parts to get us off to a flyer. Thanks to his prodigious talent it worked on a number of occasions last year. There's a big difference between losing badly and losing tamely, and we need to go out with a positive attitude and either we win by 100 runs or lose by 100 runs. None of this 'we'll see what happens', 'we'll take it down to the wire', 'wait until the last over' business. When you're on a losing run it's easy to turn up for a Sunday League game with the intention of limiting the damage, rather than searching for ways to win. I'd prefer to go all out to win, even if it means taking risks, to rekindle our interest in the remaining one-day competition. Going through the motions is not for me.

26 June - Worcestershire, Sunday League

We rested Hemmings, conserving his energy for a big day on Monday, and played young Nicky Phillips. As a portent of the day to come, I lost the toss and they elected to bat. Only Franklyn and Giddo bowled anything like and they rattled along to 243, far too many runs on that pitch, with Hick in fine form scoring over 100. Sals went for 49 in a mere six overs, Nicky Phillips for 38. A lamentable batting display left us almost 100 runs short, with Speighty the only player to make runs. We were absolutely hammered, eight out of 11 players simply failed to do their job - just not good enough. We seem to be collectively afflicted by a lack of confidence in our one-day cricket at the moment. By sending out Speighty to open the batting, with Franklyn in at three, I tried to inject some life into our performance and break out of this losing streak, but to no avail. Losing so badly again increases the pressure on us tomorrow, as the championship is the only remaining competition in which we can carry forward any impetus into the second-half of the season.

The only bright news of the day is Sals' selection for England. We are all delighted, and with the way he has bowled recently he thoroughly deserves his place. I'd like to think that the way Giffy and myself have treated him has been a contributory factor, although he has shown a great deal of fight and character to regain his form after an indifferent start to the season.

27 June - Worcestershire, final day
My worst nightmare came true today, and all I could think of whilst Hick went on relentlessly to top score with 73, and set up a victory for Worcestershire, was dropping him on nought on Saturday.

On top of the reverse sweep episode in the Nat West, and then effectively costing us a championship match by dropping Hick, I haven't enjoyed the best of weeks. Cricket is an up-and-down game and it's part of the burden of captaincy that I've learned to shoulder. The vicious circle of bad fortune will close, and the half-way point of the season provides a useful opportunity for reflection. It's certainly not satisfactory that my highest score so far has only been in the sixties, but my mind is clearly focused on a more positive run in the second part of the season.

How Sals took only one wicket today I'll never know. Franklyn bowled his heart out to take four for 78 in 31 overs, almost winning the game single-handedly. In one dramatic over he had Hick caught at mid-wicket and yorked Leatherdale for nought. At that stage they were 170 for five and I needed to rest Franklyn after a fantastic effort. There was a discussion with Sals and Peter Moores on who best to bowl next, and we decided on Giddo who has really bowled well this season. He quickly trapped Haynes lbw and removed Lampitt in the same way. For the second time, two wickets had fallen without addition to the total, and we could sense the panic in the Worcestershire batsmen, who still needed to score over 50 with only three wickets in hand. Rhodes was playing well and eventually steered them home with only one wicket left to fall, although we were convinced that he had been caught and bowled by Franklyn towards the end of the game .

The topic of batsmen walking is one often bandied about outside the game. On the circuit it's not an issue: there are batsmen who walk and there are batsmen who don't, and in my time in cricket it's never been any different. I sometimes think that the square-leg umpire could play more of a role in circumstances that are unclear to the official standing at the bowler's end. He could be consulted in the case of close decisions on bat-pads, and the ball brushing the glove, for instance. He is in a position to judge more than just run-outs and stumpings, and in some respects would be more useful than a third umpire sitting in an office watching a TV screen.

Again we bowled well enough to win the game, but our batting fell short. To see Franklyn slumped in a chair after the game, after giving his all in 31 overs, was testament to the fact that there was no shortage of commitment shown today, and the loss was a massive disappointment.

29 June - South Africa at Hove, first day
The first day of a three-day game against South Africa then a welcome 10 days off before we're back to business with a championship game against Middlesex

at Arundel. The wicket was slow and low, and our reticence to attack some mediocre bowling meant that the less than entertaining cricket did not match the game's festival atmosphere. We hobbled along at two runs an over, but it wasn't easy to score runs on the flat pitch. I shall bat on tomorrow morning, but don't expect a result, as I know Kepler Wessels is looking for batting practice.

30 June - South Africa, second day
Before the start, Giffy and Peter Moores had advised closing our innings in an attempt to make a game of it, but with three inexperienced bowlers in our side, including a debut for Jason Lewry, and Kepler playing eight recognised batsmen, I felt it wise to bat on. I instructed Jarv and Nicky Phillips to bat with caution until I sent out a message for them to attack the bowling. They took us to 310 with sensible batting, then in complete contrast to yesterday, the batsmen launched an attack against the spinner Pat Symcox, who went for 32 runs in his last two overs, before I declared. Jarv made 70, his first half-century for Sussex. It was clear that the South Africans were not over-enamoured with this tactic, but I felt justified in putting us in a safe position.

Jarv slipped into his rhythm immediately with two early wickets, and I was delighted for Jason Lewry who took Gary Kirsten's wicket in his second over in first-class cricket. Having runs on the board allowed our young bowlers to run in and bowl without pressure. Had I declared early, it might have exposed them at a critical stage of their development. Nicky Phillips also took a wicket to remember when he caught and bowled Kepler Wessels.

1 July - South Africa, final day

As I anticipated, South Africa killed the game stone dead and settled for batting practice on the final day. We were left to bat for the final session during which time we lost six wickets, and a boring game of cricket came to an unexciting and predictable close.

2 July

I seem to have a lot of people approaching me at the moment and saying things like ". . . *don't worry that things are not going as well as they should, because we still have full confidence in you and things can only get better . . .*" and other such reassuring noises, obviously referring to the runs I've scored this season, or rather the runs I haven't scored! Obviously I'm unhappy that the big scores I'm used to, and other people expect, just haven't materialised this season. Before the South African game I had made just over 500 runs, only 100 behind Billy Athey, at an average of just under 40: not disastrous, not brilliant, not particularly erratic, not setting the world alight, but a damn sight better than 250 at an average of 20. Because it hasn't happened this year, the over-concern expressed in some quarters is almost suggesting that I've had a complete disaster and forgotten how to bat. My technical ability hasn't suddenly evaporated. The difficulties are all in the mind, and I'm trying too hard for that elusive big score which you become convinced will sweep away indifferent form. It's not worrying me, but the situation does produce feelings of anxiety, and most of all frustration. The burden of expectation can be wearisome at times.

Ten days off in mid-season was punctuated by the Costcutter Cup festival in Harrogate. We actually won a one-day game by beating Yorkshire in the semi-final, always a pleasure in front of their home crowd who are never short of expectation. We met Gloucestershire in the final who were at full strength, whereas we were minus Franklyn, Sals, Eddie Hemmings, and effectively Paul Jarvis, who bowled only three overs. Courtney Walsh came in to bat with his usual flourish, swatted Keith Greenfield for a brace of sixes, and they won a very competitive game in the last over.

The break gave me plenty of time to reflect on our performances so far, and consider ways of rectifying problems for the rest of the season. If we had batted as well as we've bowled, then we would be sitting happily near the top of the championship table. Our batting has definitely lacked confidence, and has fallen some way short of expectations. In previous years, going on to 350 and more after a solid start was always on the cards, but this year it's been a case of damage limitation and an interminable struggle to reach the right side of 300. In mitigation, it is evident that many sides have bowled particularly well at us, but we have developed an uncanny knack of getting ourselves out. Regenerating our batting fortunes is a major task for the weeks ahead, and one of the things I've done is to make changes to the order. I cast my mind back to my early years in the first-team under John Barclay when we often failed to gel as a batting unit. He was not frightened to shuffle the batsmen around and promote the players in form, and those batting with confidence, higher up the order. As an experiment, Neil Lenham opened the batting in Harrogate, with Jamie Hall coming in at three. It's no good just plugging away hoping for a change of fortune. With captaincy comes the responsibility of doing the expected, but there is also an obligation not to shy away from experimenting when the situation demands a different tactic.

14 July - Middlesex at Arundel, first day

After the diversion of the tournament in Harrogate it's back to the reality of the championship, with Middlesex to face at Arundel. I won the toss, elected to bat and decided to continue with the new opening partnership of Neil Lenham and Billy Athey. The wicket looked grassy, and with the humid atmosphere I expected the ball to move around. The openers played exceptionally well and put on 93 for the first wicket. Middlesex bowled competently, and with the wicket turning as early as on the first morning, it was no surprise that the first wicket to fall was caught Tufnell bowled Emburey. I spent one hour at the crease for seven runs, fending off Phil Tufnell, and never felt as if I was about to hit him out of the attack. Scoring runs was difficult and we ended our first innings on 228, a reasonable score in the conditions. It could easily have been a lot less, with Athey dropped early on and no luck for the

Middlesex bowlers. The decision to bat looked distinctly shaky for a while, but Eddie Hemmings reminded me that you plan on the basis of what will happen over the whole match, not necessarily on what could occur in the first session.

We had forty minutes to bowl at Middlesex and in 13 penetrating overs the seamers did an excellent job. Jason Lewry, making his championship debut, took a wicket to remember by dismissing Mike Gatting, caught by the ever-reliable Peter Moores, for nought. Franklyn trapped Mike Roseberry lbw first ball and they ended the day 23 for two. The wicket and atmosphere is encouraging the ball to turn and swing, and with our balanced attack I'm looking forward to tomorrow.

Before then I have an informal dinner at Hove with the chairman, the vice-chairman, the secretary, the treasurer and the cricket manager. This is one of two informal occasions during the season when we meet to discuss the progress both the club and the team are making. It will be nice to return home to Melanie and Luke after a long drive from Harrogate to Arundel, and a taxing day's cricket.

15 July - Middlesex, second day

Before play I said to the players that we had to field and bowl as if Middlesex needed 228 (our first innings score) to win, comparing the situation to our last game at Worcester when the pressure we applied on their batsmen almost, and should have, won us the game. I wanted Middlesex to fight for every single run and the guys responded positively with a determined effort in the field. What a day! We bowled them out for 87, with fantastic performances from Franklyn and Jason Lewry. Leading up to this game I always fancied playing Jason Lewry, as the conventional seam bowler can often struggle to get anything out of the Arundel wicket. The other half of this equation was to rest Franklyn, as his bowling is not ideally suited to this type of wicket, graphically illustrated in the past at Arundel by his bouncer being taken at toe-level by Peter Moores. One implication of Franklyn not playing would be a weakened batting order, but the positive side of that might be that additional responsibility on the other batsmen, myself included, might stimulate better performances with the bat. When thinking about team selection, being able to take 20 wickets was uppermost in my mind. Franklyn was raring to go, and in the end I rested Jarv, who has a slight groin injury, in order to preserve his strength for the forthcoming games against Somerset and Surrey when his bowling will be needed on hard and bouncy wickets.

The process of 'self selection' was fully vindicated. Franklyn was on fire today and roared in to take a remarkable five for 25, his latest feat in a storming season. The debutante Lewry bowled unchanged for two hours, and ended up with four for 40 in 21 overs. For such a young and inexperienced bowler he performed impressively, never failing to pitch the ball up and use the swing. Jason has adapted very well to the demands of first-class cricket. He is learning a great deal from Jarv, who has taken him under his wing. He is also learning that the aches and pains a bowler experiences in the senior game never really go away, and Jarv has explained to him that as a fast bowler who gives it everything he cannot expect to take the field feeling 100% every time. Keith Fletcher was watching the game and I know he was impressed with Jason's performance.

Standing at slip talking to Peter Moores made me realise how much he contributes on the field. In the past he used to almost bully me into changing bowlers and adjusting the field, never the most productive way of influencing a captain, even if the idea is good. Now he is far more understanding of a captain's role and makes a major contribution beyond his wicketkeeping duties. After bowling Jason Lewry for 12 overs he was starting to show signs of tiredness, but his youthful enthusiasm was keeping him going. I was keen to take him off for a rest but Mooresy badgered me into keeping him going for a few overs more, convinced that he looked like taking a wicket every ball. His judgement was vindicated when Jason bowled a peach of a delivery to take a vital wicket with the last ball of his elongated spell. At 27 for five the heart had been ripped out of their batting order, and it was one of those days when everything went our way. They avoided the follow-on and we commenced the second innings with a lead of 141.

We lost Billy Athey's wicket with only three runs on the board, then Neil Lenham and Jamie Hall put together a useful partnership. Pin is in good form, his confidence is high and he looks like getting runs every time he comes to the wicket. Jamie Hall played a patient innings, showing solid application on a difficult pitch. On 17 I received a ball from Angus Fraser on the sort of awkward length which catches the batsman neither forward or back, and I nicked it into Gatting's hands at slip. Speighty came in and played a responsible and disciplined innings, with only the occasional flourish, ending the day on 59 not out. Watching from the pavilion, I allowed myself a wry smile as the chairman clapped in appreciation at Speighty hitting a boundary with a reverse sweep. Moorsey perished trying to cut a ball from Emburey which was too full for the shot. Having made 28, and with only three overs remaining in the day, Franklyn demonstrated the other side of his cricketing nature when he tried to smash Tufnell over mid-wicket, and skied a top edge to the keeper. It wasn't the shot I wanted to see at that stage of the game, and I sent in Eddie Hemmings ahead of Sals who I thought might be worth 20 or 30 runs the next morning. They both fell to Tufnell in quick succession and after a day when we had done so well it was galling to lose three wickets in the last three overs. Nonetheless, we have a useful lead and with Speighty still at the crease we have every chance of winning the game. When Middlesex bat tomorrow, I want to apply such pressure that their batsmen will be wondering where the next run is coming from.

I still feel concerned at my own form with the bat, but I am not distraught, as so far in this match we have performed well as a team. Watching our batsmen building up a lead was almost as pleasing as being out there doing it myself.

16 July - Middlesex, third day

My expectations of adding a further 20 runs were eclipsed by the mercurial Speighty who, in one of his whirlwind batting displays, contributed 38 of the 42 runs added to the overnight total. Yesterday he batted sensibly and this morning played the ideal mixture of defence and attack to put the match beyond Middlesex's reach. He fell a mere three runs short of the century which would have been just reward for playing the outstanding innings of the match.

The initial damage was inflicted by Franklyn, when he took the prime wickets of Haynes and Gatting for only five runs between them. Roseberry and Ramprakash counter-attacked and took Middlesex to lunch without further loss. Ed Giddins bowled a terrific spell after the break, wicketless but restricting the scoring. Eddie Hemmings had Ramprakash caught at bat-pad and I brought Sals on to bowl. He bowled magnificently, took six for 55 and we won inside three days. This convincing win should move us up the championship table, with the added bonus of results from other games involving sides above us going our way too.

Sals bowled himself into the frame for the forthcoming Test against South Africa, and although I'll miss his services if he is picked, his selection will be well-deserved. In Sals' absence, I'll need to consider whether to play a fourth seamer, or add Nicky Phillips as the second off-spinner for the game against

Somerset, depending on the state of the wicket at Hove.

David Smith is concerned that he is out of the side at the moment, having initially been left out due to injury. He played for the second-team last week and scored 80, so he naturally wants to know where he stands regarding first-team cricket, and is finding it difficult to see how he can force his way back into the side. We are due to have a serious discussion tomorrow, he obviously wants to ask some questions and I shall be nothing but honest with him. That's the way I would like to be treated and it's no good saying things just to make someone feel better. Jamie Hall has taken his chance and taken Smithy's place in the side for the moment.

I am really pleased with Giddo's progress, and as he matures, in cricketing terms, he is becoming an integral part of the team. I'm actively considering whether he should be capped towards the end of this season, especially as he has bowled so well this year. However, that carrot is currently working well as a motivator, but I'm delighted his potential is starting to be realised.

One aspect of captaincy that can't be seen from the boundary, although the results can be only too apparent if the captain fails in this regard, is the constant demands of man-management. Players have to be treated according to their needs and personalities, and it's not only newcomers to a team who need help and encouragement.

Although there's a day off on Monday to look forward to, I am hopeful that this win will lift our confidence, and provide a platform for the Sunday League fixture tomorrow.

17 July - Middlesex, Sunday League

At last a limited-overs win, and at last some runs for the captain! I spent most of the pre-match preparation telling players why they were or weren't playing, and didn't even get an opportunity to put a bat in my hands for some practice. David Smith wanted a serious chat before the game and we spent 30 minutes deep in conversation. Although I needed to pad up as I was batting at four, our discussion was too important to postpone or curtail.

Pin was injured so Jamie Hall and Speighty opened the innings, with Billy Athey scheduled to come in at five, but padded-up because I was still with Smithy. Going in at 40 for two, I made 103 to take us to 225 in the allotted overs. My first 27 runs were all in singles, and I remarked to a bemused Phil Tufnell that I was going for a Sunday League record by scoring a half-century without running more than one run at a time! I was pleased to score so many runs on such a slow wicket, and was aided by the hard-hitting Franklyn, and when he holed out by Keith Greenfield. I started to hit out later in the innings and struck two pleasing straight sixes, and an even more satisfying one off my legs, over the square-leg fence.

After losing a wicket with only one run on the board, Middlesex threatened only briefly when Ramprakash and Haynes put a useful stand together, broken by Billy Athey bowling Ramprakash with his second ball. I kept changing the bowling to keep the pressure on, and was further rewarded when Sals took a stinging return catch to dismiss Haynes. Gatting's run out effectively ended their resistance, just as he was coming to terms with the pace of the wicket, and Franklyn returned to mop up the tail by taking three wickets in five balls with superbly directed fast yorkers.

So at last a century this season, albeit in one-day cricket, and doubly satisfying because it's Melanie's birthday today and she was delighted to forgo a card in return for a century from me. John Lees of Radio Sussex came up to me after the win and congratulated me on a return to form. It doesn't make sense to me how one day you are 'out of form' and the next 'in form', but that's the way the media and public see the situation. The last time I went out to bat I scored 17, then received a good ball and the innings ended. Today I didn't even have a net or a throw-down, yet I hit a century. You don't have to be 'out of form' to get out in cricket, just as you don't necessarily have to be 'in form' to score runs. Form has little to do with technical ability, it's primarily between the ears and a matter of confidence. I'm really hoping that the big score today will spur me on to greater contributions in the remaining championship matches.

20 July
A normal Wednesday routine, although there is also a committee meeting to attend this afternoon. Nets in the morning then an examination of the wicket with Norman Gifford to formulate our strategy against

Somerset. With Sals on England duty, and Jarv back to full fitness, we need a lively wicket suited to our seam attack. If Sals isn't picked for the Test side then he will travel back to take his place in the side instead of Jason Lewry, who has a slight injury at the moment. As insurance, John North is staying behind from the second-eleven game, and as he has been scoring runs and bowling with good pace recently he comes into the twelve ahead of Carlos Remy.

In the last round of championship matches a couple of results went our way, with Leicestershire losing to Yorkshire, currently propping up the table, and Nottinghamshire losing too. For the first time in many years we are seriously studying other team's results in the second-half of the season, and working out how they impact on our own position in the championship table. All the guys are highly motivated at the moment, which makes my job slightly easier when it comes to getting the players in the right frame of mind to perform at their best. The Sunday League is a different matter, as we would have to win nearly all our remaining games to be anywhere near the prize-money positions.

21 July - Somerset at Hove, first day

The wicket has some rolled grass in it, and whether to bat or bowl first will be a difficult decision. Regardless of who wins the toss, I am confident that if we perform to our potential then we will win the game. As it was, Somerset elected to bat first and our seam bowling attack made little impression on the openers. I brought

Eddie Hemmings on first-change as the wicket ends were quite bare, and neither Trescothick or Mark Lathwell look particularly comfortable against spin. The change paid off when Trescothick was bowled around his legs. We didn't help ourselves when Billy Athey dropped Lathwell at slip, and Hemmings did the same in the gully. Both misses proved to be expensive as Lathwell went on to score 124.

For the first hour we played like championship contenders, then let them off the hook. I had a word with the guys in the changing room at lunch and stressed that we needed to be patient, hold our nerve, and make them sweat for every run, as we were having to in the field on a very hot day. Hemmings went on to make amends for the dropped catch with a vintage bowling performance, taking six for 61 in 44 overs, and restricting Somerset to 277 for seven, from a position of strength at 190 for one. I delayed taking the new ball until the last 10 minutes of play, and Ed Giddins did the trick by picking up a wicket in the last over of the day.

22 July - Somerset, second day

I decided to let Jason Lewry loose with the new ball this morning, and in his first over he removed Graham Rose with a beautiful delivery which swung very late. At 278 for eight we were set to wrap up the innings for under 300, but it was not to be and they ploughed on to 360. The subsequent tail-wagging was orchestrated by Andy Caddick, who although he has his own methods, is a handy batsman in these situations. He blocked it when the fielders were set back, and hit the ball when they were up, ending up with a useful half-century. It is so frustrating when you fail to finish a side off, as we did against Lancashire in their first innings.

I am sure that the members and the press might wonder why it took me 18 overs to bring Hemmings on to bowl, especially after his success yesterday. Franklyn was bowling into the wind and he suggested that he change ends, taking a wicket in his first over bowling down the hill and delaying the opportunity to bring back Hemmings at the end from which he took his six wickets yesterday. It would be unusual for the media to report that Hemmings' re-introduction was in fact delayed by only nine overs, as it was only ever productive to bowl him from the bottom end. I don't expect any positive comment from the press as a result of bringing on a spinner first-change on the first morning of a championship game. All credit to Eddie for taking the wickets, but the captain has to be enterprising enough to take a chance.

Billy Athey and Neil Lenham again got us off to a good start but we ended the day on a disappointing 256 for seven. Harvey Trump, their off-spinner, bowled well and was sending the ball down at a slower pace than I remember, making it difficult to score freely. Shortly after tea I was caught down the leg side and worse was to follow in the next over when Speighty fell in the same manner. Jamie Hall and Franklyn batted well together, and their contrasting styles were illustrated by Franklyn blazing away to push the field back, then getting caught off one big shot too many trying to clear the field, rather than finding the gaps for ones and twos. Jamie Hall chased a wide ball in the last over and was caught behind, so having made a recovery to 255 for five, we again undermined our position by throwing away two wickets late in the day and handing the initiative back to Somerset. The wicket is now turning at both ends, and if Mark Lathwell can pick up a couple of wickets there is no reason why Billy Athey, another occasional bowler, shouldn't do the same for us. I'll be looking for a major contribution from Eddie Hemmings to restrict Somerset when they bat again, to help leave us with an achievable target to win the game.

I'm continually aware that for the team to become more consistent as a batting side, and knock off big scores in the last innings to win games, I have to be contributing more in terms of runs. This run of low scores is also detrimental to my waistline as I'm eating far more ice-creams in the pavilion than I've ever done in my career. At least I've been able to watch some Test cricket, and having toured South Africa with Steve Rhodes, Darren Gough and John Crawley, it's satisfying to see them playing for England. I felt nervous for John Crawley watching him bat, and although he was obviously more relieved than I was when he got off the mark, I was pleased to see the start of his Test career.

23 July - Somerset, third day
We added very few runs to our overnight score and were bowled out in little more than seven overs. Nothing seemed to work in the morning session, and by lunch they were 105 without loss off 25 overs, with

Lathwell and Trescothick scoring freely. In the middle session I concentrated on defensive fields and damage limitation. Franklyn even bowled some off-spin and eventually accounted for Lathwell, denying him a century by eight runs. Jarv put his heart and soul into his bowling, almost getting a hat-trick after blowing away Harden and Hayhurst in successive balls. He continued to steam in relentlessly after tea and by the end of the day he was rewarded with seven for 58, close to his career best of seven for 55. He was looking like cleaning up the tail-enders but had to leave the field with a groin strain. It was the sort of display we all know Jarv is capable of: fast and accurate. Eddie Hemmings had left the field earlier after picking up an injury, along with a bit of a pasting from Trescothick, which left me reliant on seam on a wicket conducive to spin. With my two wicket takers in the pavilion we struggled to end their innings and Caddick, again showing he is no mug with the bat, put on 49 with Trump and they declared leaving us a stiff target of 383 to win. I was puzzled that they appeared to be batting without purpose, rather than going all out for some extra runs once a position of safety had been secured. There was nothing to lose, and in that position I would have sent out an instruction for some lusty blows before declaring.

It's frustrating to be chasing the game against Somerset. Although they have some useful cricketers, we are more than a match for them and it's a game I would expect to win. If we're outplayed then I can accept that, but to place ourselves in a vulnerable position through our own mistakes is galling, and a situation I'm determined to rectify. Our problems in this game are all self-inflicted.

24 July - Somerset, Sunday League

I was annoyed to read a match report in the Daily Telegraph asserting that Jarv's spell of seven wickets was basically futile, as Somerset were going to win anyway. Far from it. He kept us in the game with his bowling and without Jarv's efforts we would be facing an impossible 450. Reading ill-informed press reports like this makes me wonder sometimes whether some reporters know what the game is about.

I had to make a few changes to the one-day side: Lewry, Hemmings and Jarv were out with injuries, and Sals is on England duty. I also played Smithy in place of Jamie Hall, which was a little hard on Jamie but I needed extra stability and experience at the top of the order. It's never easy to omit a player from the team when he is basically performing well, but every week I have to pick a side which I think is right to win the game for Sussex. Naturally Jamie was upset but I felt Smithy was the right choice for this game.

I put them in and thanks to a combination of some tight bowling and indifferent batting they finished with 157. Nicky Phillips bowled exceptionally well to take two for 19 off his eight overs, a really good effort for a young off-spinner. John North and Carlos Remy also did well on a flat wicket offering little more than the prospect of hard work to the bowler. It's pleasing when young players who aren't regulars in the first-team come in and perform so well. It illustrates the strength in depth we have at Sussex and demonstrates that we have some bright prospects for the years ahead.

It would have been easy to open with Smithy and Billy Athey, to get us of to a steady start and set up a platform to win the game. I decided on the more adventurous tactic of opening with Smithy, to play the anchor role, and giving Speighty a brief to hit out. Franklyn would come in at three, to ensure that our innings wouldn't lack momentum. Speighty was out early on, but Franklyn put us on the road to victory. My preference for Smithy was justified as he guided the side to victory with 54 not out. It was interesting to note that Somerset looked an ordinary side, and once Franklyn got going their heads went down, and the game was ours. This bodes well for tomorrow, providing of course we bat well enough to gain the upper hand.

25 July - Somerset, final day

The team-talk focused on the necessity for the batsman to believe that with gritty determination and application we can win the game, and move towards striking distance of the top three in the table. It's a big target but we will only have ourselves to blame if we fail to come away with 22 points. I want a session by session approach to our batting today, with the emphasis on preserving wickets for a final assault.

The openers lead by example and put on 75 for the first wicket. The nature of Billy Athey's dismissal made me feel that luck might not be with us today. He hit a full-blooded pull off Harvey Trump straight at short square-leg, and somehow the ball lodged under the fielder's armpit or somewhere equally ridiculous as he was taking evasive action. Jamie Hall came in, and in partnership with Neil Lenham, saw us through to lunch without further loss.

In the next session, Neil Lenham was out for a fine 73 and I was out for a third-ball duck, leaving us on 158 for three. I misjudged the length of a ball from Harvey Trump, and instead of playing back I went forward and was caught at bat-pad. Speighty scored a whirlwind 48 then inexplicably holed-out to deep square-leg. Once again he had dismembered the field, and the bowlers were at his mercy to be knocked around into the gaps. After a composed and assured second half-century of the game, Jamie Hall pushed at an off-cutter from Graham Rose, and was bowled through the gate. Moorsey put up some typical resistance, but straight after tea Rose took his wicket with a good return catch. Franklyn lives by the sword and unfortunately dies by it too, and was out trying to hit over mid-on. Jarv was last out for a spirited 26, and we lost the game by 68 runs.

I felt that we had an excellent chance of winning this game, and after my exhortations to the batsmen before play started I was bitterly disappointed not to contribute anything with the bat. I have to look back and accept that as a batsman I didn't do my job. The difference between winning and losing was one half-decent knock from the captain, and I failed to deliver.

27 July

I played for Jack Russell's Rest of the World XI versus Gloucestershire Greats in a benefit game for Jack at Cheltenham today. I was fortunate to discuss the art of batting with Alvin Kallicharran, who asked me how my season was progressing. I explained that I wasn't scoring the runs I had hoped for, and he asked me to run through how I had been dismissed. After telling him I have been caught in my last four innings he said immediately that I wasn't watching the ball closely enough. It struck me as a strange diagnosis at first, but I recall how David Gower and Desmond Haynes were both advised that not watching the ball was the cause of bad spells they went through.

Kallicharran explained the difference between watching the bowler run in to you, and actually concentrating on watching the ball in the bowler's hand, from the moment he turns to bowl. When I watch the bowler running in I am looking at a zone around his head and arm. If you fail to focus solely on the ball, then I can appreciate how you are missing the crucial part of the delivery. Although on the face of it, watching the ball is such a fundamental part of batting, I can see the difference between the two techniques. I tried it out in the benefit game and found that the act of concentration itself cleared the mind.

28 July - Surrey at The Oval, first day

After the loss to Somerset, it is imperative that we get back on course with a strong performance, and I reiterated this to the team before play. Fighting back to beat the championship leaders, after a hiccup against a weaker team, with all respect to Somerset, will be a true test of our ability and will to win.

The wicket looked green and I expected to be inserted if I lost the toss. For this reason I was looking for a little more depth to our batting and decided to play Carlos Remy instead of Jason Lewry. The start was delayed due to rain, the wicket was damp and the outfield slow, so on winning the toss I didn't hesitate to put Surrey in to bat.

Franklyn ran in like a man possessed and took the prize wicket of Alec Stewart for a duck. He then had Darren Bicknell caught by Sals who is rapidly becoming an accomplished slip fielder. Further success followed when Sals took another catch off Franklyn's bowling to dismiss Ward, and they were rocking on 55 for three. I then had to rest Franklyn, and the pressure subsided as they wrested back the initiative. Graham Thorpe batted well and looked hungry for runs. He obviously has one eye on the Headingley Test next week, and rightly so as surely he can't be overlooked again.

After lunch Jarv broke the recovery partnership by removing Brown, and they lost their last six wickets for 34 runs. The turning point was when Franklyn came back into the attack and Jamie Hall took a blinding catch at extra cover, high to his left like a goalkeeper, to dismiss Thorpe. When Tony Pigott came in it felt very strange to be standing at slip with Lester batting, having spent so many years together in the same side. Nonetheless, I wanted him out as quickly as possible, and Franklyn obliged, assisted by a diving catch by

Mooresy. Neil Lenham brilliantly ran-out Joey Benjamin and the innings ended with everything going our way. Franklyn took six for 50. He always retained control and bowled intelligently, allowing the wicket to do the work. It was just the sort of performance I needed from him, as Jarv was carrying an injury, Giddo was out of sorts, and Carlos Remy is still learning at this level. We lost two early wickets and in the gathering gloom I faced the additional challenge of not losing my wicket to Lester, who was fired up after dismissing Billy Athey.

29 July - Surrey, second day

At last Sussex break a record. Jamie Hall took 304 minutes to score his half-century and beat a championship record which has stood since 1889! He took some stick in the dressing room, but in the circumstances he did an excellent job giving our first innings the stability it needed for us to reach a lead of 149. Brian Lara has a bat with 501 on the face, and Graham Gooch has 333. Courtesy of a bit of handiwork by Sals, Jamie Hall has white tape wrapped round the face of his bat saying 304 - with 'minutes' in small print.

Everyone chipped in with some runs, and I was particularly pleased with 66 from Moorsey, and a classy knock from Carlos Remy batting at eight. Giddo walked to the crease with Carlos three short of his fifty and he hung around long enough for Carlos to reach 55 not out. I was pleased that the selection of Carlos worked out, as the last thing tired bowlers want to see is a genuine batsman coming in at eight. It is the first time we've batted a full day in the championship this year and I was delighted with the patience and application shown by the players. I was out cheaply to a brilliant diving catch by Alec Stewart, and although nothing seems to be going my way as a batsman, I take some solace from an excellent team performance. Billy Athey reminded me that form is something which comes and goes but class remains. It's the sort of comment and support I need to help me through this difficult spell.

For some reason we were staying in a hotel in Hampstead, and some of the players took the underground to and from the ground. Franklyn Stephenson often brings his guitar to the ground, and is always on hand to revitalise the side at breaks in play by strumming away. On this occasion, he was on the way back to the hotel by tube with Sals and Moorsey. Sals decided on a spot of impromptu busking and took off his jacket to place on the ground to collect the coins in front of a guitar-playing Franklyn. I'm not sure to what degree they managed to enhance the county cricketer's wage, but Franklyn earned a new nickname - *The Busker*.

30 July - Surrey, third day
An extraordinary session and I could not be happier with the team's performance. Franklyn bowled magnificently for the whole session, and his five for 32 gave him memorable match figures of 11 for 82. Jarv took some punishment from Thorpe, but he also took three wickets, including the two openers. Giddo chipped in with two, including the final wicket 15

minutes after the scheduled time for lunch. The carnage took less than 28 overs, and Surrey were all out for 115, losing by an innings and 34 runs. The Surrey batsmen didn't help themselves but the bowling was good enough to invite them to play at balls they might have left alone.

I can't remember the last time we beat Surrey at The Oval, and to annihilate them in only seven sessions is a great result. The atmosphere in the dressing room was euphoric, and I'm now off to Smithy's for a barbecue and a well-earned celebration in the sunshine.

31 August - Surrey, Sunday League

Surrey exacted a measure of revenge for their championship defeat, on a wicket bordering on the dangerous. It was either bouncy or extremely bouncy, even off the medium pacers, but we managed to reach 186 batting first. We lost quick wickets forcing the pace and it was only thanks to Mooresy that we managed a decent score.

Surrey made more of batting on the wicket and we never made serious inroads into their batting. To put the brakes on, I experimented with bowling changes, and seeing that Ward and Hollioake were about to get after Sals, I took him off rather than be left solely with the option of taking remedial action. Franklyn and Jason Lewry had a couple of overs each to quieten things down, with the effect of raising the runs needed per over to nearly eight, and bringing a new batsman to the crease. I then brought Sals back on for his final three overs, and but for a dropped catch we might have been in with a chance. They managed to slog Sals for 30 runs and overhauled our total to win the game.

Sunday is a hectic day for the captain. We always take extra players to cover for injuries and to give me a choice when it comes to final team selection. My preparation is given over to rushing around talking to players and sorting out the tactics with Giffy. Against Surrey, Nicky Phillips found out he wasn't playing before I had time to talk to him about it, when the team was announced over the tannoy .

3 August

Nets today before we travel to play Northamptonshire. I had a fitness test on an elbow injury before I left Hove, and although I should be able to bat without too many problems, I can't throw the ball. I can pick from a full-strength squad, and the team will be joined by Jason Lewry, who having been sent up to Old Trafford from our last game at The Oval to play for the second- team will now travel back down to Northampton to join the first-team. In his first year on the staff he's learning a lot about the link between motorway travel and the life of a professional cricketer.

The wicket at Northampton is usually prepared to suit seam bowling, but I'll have to reserve any decisions on our bowling attack until I've seen the pitch and a weather forecast.

4 August - Northamptonshire at Northampton, first day

Much as we anticipated, the wicket was green and there

was rain in the air. Our team selection was thrown into turmoil with the loss of Jamie Hall to a rib injury sustained in a morning net session. Carlos Remy retained his place and Jason Lewry came in instead of Eddie Hemmings, as a second spinner isn't needed on this wicket. I moved up to bat at three and Carlos bolstered the middle order at five.

Northants put us in and the openers got us off to a good start, never easy on this sort of wicket against Ambrose and Curran. I was out for 16, hooking Ambrose down to fine leg, and Speighty was lbw for two. Although I didn't score many runs I felt confident enough to have a go at Ambrose, and took that as a positive improvement in my batting. Carlos Remy and Moorsey batted us back into a good position, much as they did against Surrey, then Franklyn joined Carlos for the best partnership of the match. Again Carlos looked a competent and confident prospect. He creates time to play the pace bowlers, avoids the bouncer very well, and demonstrated a good range of shots in his 60. Franklyn played his normal positive game, and was 64 not out in a total of 256 for eight, a good effort on this wicket after being asked to bat first.

The play reminded me of the game against Somerset at Hove. Apart from when Ambrose had the ball in his hand, there was very little evidence that Northants were trying to generate a positive atmosphere. I don't think it's that Sussex are suddenly a more demonstrative side, but creating pressure situations has been a feature of our cricket this season, and you really notice it when other teams appear to lack passion and commitment. They are blooding some youngsters in the side and I fancy that if we get on top of them the game will be ours.

5 August - Northamptonshire, second day

Franklyn failed to add to his overnight score but Jason Lewry and Giddo added 17 for the last wicket. It doesn't sound a lot, but on an uneven wicket every run is vital. Franklyn then launched a devastating spell of bowling, blowing away the Northants top order. After seven blistering overs during which he took two wickets, he was looking for a rest, but a wicket by Jason Lewry at the other end helped me convince him to keep going. In his next over Franklyn bowled an absolute snorter to remove Mal Loye, caught behind by Moorsey, and Montgomery went the same way moments later. Giddo carried on the good work and at lunch they were floundering on 80 for seven. After lunch Giddo carried on where he left off, and although they narrowly avoided the follow-on we had a lead of 129. Franklyn had a slight hamstring pull and I was hoping Giddo would polish off the tail. However, once they had passed the follow-on target, and I knew Franklyn could soon enjoy a rest, I brought him back to take the last wicket and end with five for 22, taking him past 50 wickets for the season.

Overnight we reached 153 for two, myself and Speighty returning to form with a partnership of 116. With two days left we are in the driving seat, and set to claim 22 more championship points.

Franklyn has been nothing short of inspirational this

season, and Giddo seems to have been spurred on in the wake of some awesome bowling. If this is Franklyn's retort to Sussex's acquisition of the Barbadian Vaspert Drakes, then he couldn't have come up with a better response. I have never known him produce so many commanding performances with bat and ball. As we approach the end of the season, player's contracts come up for discussion and one burning issue at the moment is the retention of Franklyn. I have no doubts in my mind and will present a strong case to the committee to retain him in the side for next year. This might present a difficulty with Vaspert Drakes, as he is obviously very keen to play first-class cricket. Vaspert has a good chance of touring with the West Indies next year, so he might not be available for the whole season anyway. He is under contract with us next year, although he isn't yet registered with Sussex, as we can only register one overseas player. My suggestion is to pay him a decent enough retainer to demonstrate our good faith and reassure him that we want him as our overseas player when Franklyn finishes his career at Sussex. We have worked hard on building team spirit this year, and we have discovered winning ways. Even if we don't win the championship this year, I am loath to do anything to affect our chances next year, when we shall certainly be close contenders again.

6 August - Northamptonshire, third day
We batted on and I was delighted to score 62. Again I caused my own downfall, this time run out, but I felt

positive throughout and confident of scoring runs. As the lead built up towards 400 the batsman hit out to force the pace, none as effectively as the mighty Franklyn, who in the course of scoring his second half-century of the match, took their young leg-spinner apart with some brutal hitting.

We were always in control, and it was a matter of time before we took the 10 wickets required for victory. Franklyn opened the bowling but this time Giddo stole the limelight. Jarv set us up by removing Bailey and Lamb in an impressively fast spell to claim his piece of the action. Giddo broke up a threatening fourth-wicket stand between Montgomerie and Mal Loye, followed by the wicket of Curran, all in the space of four overs, to finish with superb figures of four for 20. Sals and Franklyn mopped up the last four wickets between them, and we recorded our third win inside three days in four matches.

The Northants players later admitted that we produced the best bowling they have faced this year, and it's no secret that I think we have the most balanced attack on the circuit. Confidence is sky-high and it's a new feeling to be facing the run-in to the end of the season with high hopes and expectations.

7 August - Northamptonshire, Sunday League
I'm resting Franklyn for this game and need the day off myself as my elbow is still sore, and leaves me in no state to play a one-day game. Billy Athey will captain the side and John North will come in for Franklyn.

The wicket had a slightly corrugated surface and it was hard to score runs. Northants surpassed our total of 152 with two overs to spare, and our dismal run of Sunday League performances goes on.

11 August - Derbyshire at Eastbourne, first day

The wicket is fairly dry and the ends look bare enough to be exploited by the spinners. Jamie Hall is out injured, so Smithy comes back in. I won the toss and decided to bat, but the weather allowed only 14 overs to be bowled and we reached 27 for one. Derbyshire appear to be more interested in the Sunday League, but this will still be a tough game to win.

12 August - Derbyshire, second day

This is now effectively a three-day game and we shall have to play it accordingly. At the start I was looking for a total of 200-plus, but we slumped to 171, our lowest score of the season. DeFreitas moved the ball off the seam and in the air, thoroughly deserving his five wickets. Malcolm was also hard to manage and he took four for 37. Smithy held the innings together for most of the day to score 63.

Our backs were to the wall and I demanded accurate bowling and pressure cricket from the team. Franklyn and Jarv bowled too straight if anything and most of the 53 runs we conceded before tea were on the leg side. The atmosphere was flat and the game was threatening to slip away. Giddo made a breakthrough in his first over after tea when I caught Peter Bowler at slip. Sals and Giddo then switched ends to give the seamer a breeze at his back. Sals bowled Adams in his first over with a classic leg-spin delivery, and Giddo continued unchanged to take five for 38 in an inspired spell. Sals took four for 30 and they crashed to 123 all out, leaving us with an unexpected lead of 48.

When our openers went out to bat, Moorsey encouraged the whole team onto the balcony to offer visible support, along with Giffy and Chris Waller. His action typified our togetherness this season, in that the guys need no prompting from me to rally round the team. Billy Athey and Neil Lenham survived an uncomfortable 10 overs, with the ball still moving around.

Even though the situation was tense, there was still time for a bout of humour. Sals bowled Tim O'Gorman with what he admitted was basically a long-hop, which unexpectedly skidded on and trapped O'Gorman lbw. In the post-wicket gathering it was suggested that if Shane Warne had bowled such a delivery, Richie Benaud would be acclaiming the deadly flipper. Without a moment's hesitation Franklyn chipped in and declared that Sals' ball, which slipped out of his hand, would henceforth be known as the 'slipper'.

Giddo is bowling so well at the moment that he is the first name on the team sheet, whether we're playing a championship game or a Sunday League fixture. For me it's an unequivocal sign that it's time for him to be awarded his county cap, and I'll be talking to Giffy about arranging it.

13 August - Derbyshire, third day

One result of our good cricket this season has been other counties have had to look at our results, and it is a welcome change to be considered a threat. To be feared gives you a psychological advantage in cricket, and one I am always ready to exploit.

The euphoria of yesterday wilted under some determined bowling from the Derbyshire seamers, particularly from Dominic Cork who took six for 29 to bundle us out for 127. If it wasn't for Speighty we would have struggled to make 100. Our lead of 176 is going to take all of our resources to defend. I nicked a leg side loosener off Malcolm to the keeper and considered myself unlucky to lay a bat on it. I felt the frustration of the crowd as I walked off, and realised that as far as they see it I was again out for a low score when a captain's innings was needed.

When we bowled, the team again demonstrated their fighting qualities and the bowlers responded to make run scoring a perilous exercise. By the close of play they had reached 94 for five and a nail-biting finish is in prospect for Monday.

14 August - Derbyshire, Sunday League

Another Sunday, another one-day defeat. With our inexperienced bowling attack, losing the toss was always going to give us problems. I played Alex Edwards, a teenager who came on the pre-season tour with us. He's not even on the staff so he was delighted to play and gain some experience.

After the game I went into one of the corporate

hospitality marquees and a disgruntled businessman quizzed me at length regarding my team selection for today. He made it clear that he had not spent good money entertaining his guests for them to see a below-strength side. His disappointment at not seeing any of the five front line bowlers was sufficient for him to suggest that a letter expressing his disgust would be finding its way to the chairman.

Hemmings doesn't play Sunday League anyway, Giddo had a touch of flu, and Franklyn had a slight hamstring pull which I didn't want to risk, so I only rested two out of five. The general reaction was as if I'd given the whole team a day off! If we were in contention for one of the top spots in the Sunday League, I might have played Franklyn, but I felt it more prudent, and certainly in Sussex's best interests, to rest him ready for the final day of the championship game. I deliberated over the decision all Saturday evening, weighing up the pros and cons of various permutations. I could never forgive myself if I had risked a bowler for a Sunday League game only for him to sustain an injury which could jeopardise the possibility of Sussex winning the championship for the first time in history.

15 August - Derbyshire at Eastbourne, final day

We have to take five wickets for under 82 runs to win. At least one hour before the start of play Franklyn had marked out his run up and was almost pawing at the ground in anticipation. Eddie Hemmings took one look at him, turned to me and said *"Give the ball to the big fella."* Franklyn stormed in from the start and in his second over knocked over the obstinate Karl Krikken. DeFreitas threatened with a brisk 14 and the seventh wicket fell with Derbyshire still 58 runs adrift. As the runs mounted I took Eddie Hemmings off and brought on Giddo. With his first two deliveries he removed Cork and Warner. With Giddo on a hat-trick, 28 runs needed to win, nine wickets down and Devon Malcolm at the crease, the atmosphere was electric. I thought of bowling Hemmings from the other end, but decided to back Franklyn to knock Devon Malcolm over. As you would expect from Devon he managed to swipe and miss at everything wide of the stumps yet somehow managed to connect with the straight ones. Franklyn tried his legendary slower ball, and twice deceived the batsman. In one crucial over Malcolm did spot the slower ball and launched it out of the park for six. After a heart-stopping period of play, Derbyshire won the game by one wicket. Kim Barnett was as amazed as I was at Malcolm's match-winning display with the bat.

Coming off the field I felt as numb as when we lost the Nat West final last season. The feeling of desolation is hard to articulate. On one level you just can't believe what's happened, and the closing scenes rush through your mind, almost being willed into a different ending. When Giddo took two wickets in successive deliveries I was convinced that the game was won. Franklyn observed that this season is rapidly becoming the year that could have been, with the team being denied wins at the death: 10 runs short at Notts, one wicket short at Worcester, Devon Malcolm batting Derbyshire to victory. If we had won just two of those games then Sussex would be heading the championship. It doesn't bear thinking about.

With a crunch game against Leicestershire to come there is no time to dwell over what might have been, as we will need every effort to stay in contention.

17 August

Keith Greenfield and Carlos Remy have joined the eleven who played at Eastbourne. Jamie Hall is fit again but he hasn't batted for three weeks, allowing Smithy back in the side. I expect a green wicket, rather than one helpful to our spinners, so Carlos is here as the fourth seamer, as well as being a useful addition to the batting line-up.

On a result pitch there will be no shortage of wickets, so putting adequate runs on the board will be essential to win the match. If the wicket is exceptionally green I might be tempted to leave out Sals and play Keith Greenfield as an extra batsman. There would have to be exceptional circumstances for me not to play a spinner at all, as I am committed to variation in the bowling attack. You can't call a bowler on when he's sitting in the pavilion having been left out the side. Bowling has been the least of our problems this season. Looking back at the three games we should have won, a lack of runs has been our downfall. Brian Lara has scored more centuries this season than Sussex players have.

Leicester holds fond memories for me. In the early eighties I came here in a side with Imran, Garth le Roux,

Ian Grieg and so on. I had scored a few runs in the game prior and the captain promoted me in the order, whereas I was normally coming in at five or six. Coming in at three I scored my first first-class hundred, against a useful attack. I remember it not only because it was an important milestone in my career, but because it reminds me of how to get the best out of young players, especially when their confidence is high. In 1990 I was asked to be acting captain of a young side at Leicester when Paul Parker was injured. Against the odds we beat Leicestershire and I scored another century.

18 August - Leicestershire at Grace Road, first day
Leicestershire are above us in the table and have a game in hand, so we have to win this game. After a long look at the wicket, and discussions with Giffy and the senior players, I decided to reverse my earlier thoughts on selection and play both spinners. We lost the toss and they decided to bat, on a wicket with a green tinge. Both sides expect the wicket to wear badly, as is normally the case at Leicester, so I would have batted first had I had the choice.

In the first session we didn't bowl particularly well, and sent down too many loose deliveries on a wicket with pace and bounce. What struck me was the lack of atmosphere, no apparent recognition of the fact that this is a big game for us. At lunch I admonished the players and made it clear that we didn't look like a side challenging for the championship, and that had to change when we went back on the field. They needed reminding that if we let Leicestershire boss the game then we will lose, and that's effectively the end of our season. I wanted to feel the effort and commitment in the air, create some pressure and make things happen. The second session was more like the pressure cricket we have applied this season, and we bowled them out for under 200. We finished the day 57 for one, with Smithy out for nought and Billy Athey retiring hurt having been struck on the elbow by a ball from David Millns.

19 August - Leicestershire, second day

We have had some exciting days cricket this year but none as gripping and as satisfying as today, when we comprehensively beat Leicestershire inside two days. We started aiming to bat on all day and amass a big score. Neil Lenham scored a good half-century and I fell four short at 46. With both teams straining every sinew the atmosphere was heady, and the Leicestershire players were very combative. Neil Lenham survived an appeal for a caught behind, much to David Millns obvious disgust, and there was further exasperation for the bowlers when Vince Wells bowled the same batsman with a no-ball. This was clearly too much for Alan Mullally, who after directing one or two well chosen words at me, was reprimanded by umpire Ray Julian. We passed their first innings score with five wickets in hand but then collapsed to take a lead of only 55, our last eight batsmen going for less than 100 runs. The pitch was basically sound, but it was offering help to bowlers prepared to put the ball in the right place.

At tea I said to the players that although we hadn't gained the lead we had hoped for, there was every chance of running through a fragile middle order once the top batsmen were out of the way. I felt that the key was to expose the middle order to the new ball, stressing the fact that if the bowlers kept to a disciplined line and length we could make serious inroads into their batting in the 48 overs available to us before the close of play.

They were skittled out for 90 in less than 40 overs. Franklyn was again magnificent. He reeled off 16 overs of skill and variety, using the new ball brilliantly to take four for 23. Jarv also took four wickets and the spinners shared the balance. The wicket taken by Eddie Hemmings was the 1,500th of his career, a special moment for him and a privilege for the team to witness this fantastic feat. With only 36 needed to win I claimed the extra half-hour and the 21 points were ours. If results of the other matches go in our favour then we're back in the hunt, thanks to a good all-round team performance.

21 *August - Leicestershire, Sunday League*

In contrast to last week there was no justification to play less than a full-strength side. Keith Greenfield, John North and Carlos Remy came in to replace Neil Lenham, David Smith and Eddie Hemmings. The Sunday League is a lost cause for us now, but I wanted the players to give it everything, and drive back down the motorway with a one-day win to add to the championship points we had worked so hard to earn.

It was a good performance for the team and for me personally. We were again shaky after losing the first wicket, but I managed to hold things together and stayed in for almost 30 overs to score 51, with wickets falling at the other end. Jarv and Sals hit some lusty blows at the death and fittingly the last ball of our 40 overs was smacked for six by Sals, to give us a total of 205.

After losing three wickets with the score static on 21, they never looked like threatening our total and we won the game by 42 runs to complete an excellent few days for Sussex and a miserable time for Leicestershire.

As I was leaving the field, the twelfth man passed me a message asking me to telephone Ray Illingworth. My immediate thought was that he wanted to ask me about the form of one or two Sussex players. I was surprised and thrilled to be offered the job of leading England A to India this winter. After an indifferent season with the bat I had feared that the A tour to South Africa last winter might have been it as far as England recognition was concerned. To be offered the captaincy made me feel that all my efforts over the years haven't been in vain, and it keeps my England ambitions alive. The good memories of Leicester continue.

25 August - Warwickshire at Hove, first day
The day started ominously with heavy rain. The wicket is grassy and damp having sweated under the covers. I'd dearly love to beat Warwickshire, not only to close the gap in the championship but to avenge the Nat

West defeat last season.

When the covers first came off the wicket it was quite moist and at that stage I fancied bowling first. The sun came out and the wicket appeared to dry quickly, so I changed my mind and decided to bat. Neil Lenham was out early on but the real damage was inflicted in one over from Roger Twose, when he took the wickets of Billy Athey, myself and Martin Speight. Gladstone Small and Tim Munton brushed aside any remaining resistance and we were all out for a pathetic 131. They sent in a nightwatchman to open instead of Roger Twose and Franklyn knocked him over first ball. Twose then came in only to be bowled by Jarv, so at nine for two there is still a game on.

My biggest fear when I took over the captaincy was how would I cope if I lost form and the runs dried up. Thankfully that didn't happen in the first two years but it has now. A captain's nightmare is poor form leading to a loss of effectiveness in leading the team. Despite my lack of achievements with the bat, I have a firm grip of what we are trying to achieve as a team and feel my leadership and desire to see Sussex win has not been diminished in any way. I have the energy, enthusiasm and will to win for the team, even though I am failing in my individual performances.

26 August - Warwickshire, second day

Conflicting emotions today. At one stage we looked like clawing our way back into the match, found ourselves facing the ignominy of losing inside two days, and eventually ended up precariously placed with a wholly inadequate lead of 55, and only two wickets remaining.

Andy Moles mistimed a hook off the first ball of the day and was brilliantly caught by Billy Athey. Lara then entered the arena. Keith Piper, the second nightwatchman, was next to go when he was caught by Sals off Jarv. Giddo, hurling himself down the hill from the Cromwell Road end, gave no quarter to Lara, who is no different to any other left-hander in that he thrives off width. He offered a simple return catch to Giddo, who true to form spurned the opportunity in favour of having him caught at slip by Sals three balls later. With Warwickshire reduced to 67 for five we were clawing our way back in the game. Dominic Ostler played well, with the ball seaming and swinging around, and he helped Warwickshire take a lead of 52. Eventually Ostler was dismissed to give Giddo his 50th wicket of the season. I was mindful of the last match against Leicestershire, when we took a similar lead then ran through their batting to win inside two days. Surely the same couldn't happen to us, but my worst fears were realised in the second innings when our championship hopes were blown apart.

Towards the close of the Warwickshire innings I was considering the options open to me to force Sussex back into contention. Given that we had to win, I decided that attack was the best option, calculating that a psychological as well as tactical advantage could be obtained by wiping off their lead as quickly and as positively as possible. I had been encouraged by a couple of overs from Sals and thought that a target of 200 or so in the last innings would be far from a formality with our bowlers to face on this pitch. I discussed my plan with Franklyn as we left the field, and we decided that he would go in at three with a mission to cancel out the lead.

Neil Lenham was out for one, then Franklyn was bowled by Munton without even laying bat on ball, let alone mounting an attack. Regardless of how badly things turn out, I never regret taking this type of risk as it is always carefully considered and implemented with positive intent. When Billy Athey fell just after tea there was a growing atmosphere of doom, accompanied by a stark realisation that our championship hopes were fading. He was reluctant to leave the crease when he appeared to edge a delivery to slip, surely more to do with his own reluctance to accept that the end was nigh rather than to dispute the decision. Inexplicably I fenced at a ball at least 10 inches wide of off stump, and was caught behind off Twose for the second time in the match. It was such a weak and innocuous dismissal that I was kicking myself all the way back to the pavilion, thinking that as long as I played shots like that I didn't deserve to win anything.

At the end of the season I know that I'll look back on the events of today and realise that it was then that we lost all hope of going for the championship. Despite the feelings of intense disappointment we have learned valuable lessons this season which will stand us in good stead next year. We have learned how to win, and we know how to take 20 wickets to win a game. At times the bowling has been inspirational. Ed Giddins has typified our belief in controlled bowling, with the

right mix of raw pace and experimentation. He is sharp
enough to bowl a fast bouncer every over, but has taken
50 wickets for the first time in his career with
disciplined performances where pressure has been as
important as pace. It is unbelievably frustrating that not
one Sussex batsman has performed consistently with
the bat, unless you count low scores as a perverse form
of consistency! On paper, our batting is formidable,
with the right blend of experience and natural talent:
David Smith, Billy Athey, Neil Lenham, Jamie Hall,
Martin Speight, and myself. It looks as if for the first
time in my career at Sussex we will finish the season
without a batsman scoring 1000 runs. We've
experimented with the wicket at Hove, producing a
track suited to our seam attack, but this has also helped
our opponents. Maybe next year we'll shave all the
grass off and make it the domain of our spinners, who
in my mind are the best pairing in the country.

27 August - Warwickshire, third day

The miracle we needed to save the game failed to
materialise and we lost. The guys were resigned to
losing today, so the sense of disappointment is not as
acute as yesterday. Despite this defeat, the team now
believes that they are capable of beating any other side
in the championship, and although we have two games
to go, when no effort will be spared to earn maximum
points, there is already a feeling of optimism for next
year.

There was an ex-players reunion at the ground today
and it proved to be more entertaining than the cricket

which had preceded it. Ted Dexter, John Langridge and Rupert Webb were present, along with people from the more recent past such as Peter Graves, Jerry Groom and Roger Marshall. Some of us retired to the squash club bar afterwards where Jerry Groom, who was the second-eleven captain when I first joined the staff, held court and entertained us all in grand style with stories from the past. He had fun telling the guys how he talked me through my first second-eleven century at Nottingham. Dermot Reeve was also there and he had us in stitches with his impersonation of Imran Khan.

28 August - Warwickshire, Sunday League
If anyone is going to stop Warwickshire winning all four competitions I'd like it to be us. I honestly believe that although such a feat would be a stupendous achievement for Warwickshire, it would illustrate an imbalance in our domestic cricket and not necessarily be good for the game.

Another Jekyll and Hyde performance from us failed to prevent Warwickshire marching on to the Sunday League title. Compared to last week when we really got it together against Leicestershire, today we were abysmal. We played on the same wicket as the championship game, although it was cut a lot closer, and we hobbled along to a very poor 158 and were never in the game. Again I had to play a holding role, and could never unleash my natural game as the other end was too unstable. I was disappointed that there was an end of term approach from some of the guys, and even though it can be hard to motivate yourself at this stage of the season, I will not tolerate a lackadaisical attitude whether it's the first or last game of the season. Giving your all in every game is an important part of the process of becoming a winning side, one hungry for success, one prepared to determine it's own destiny rather than be at the mercy of others.

To give Warwickshire their due, they are a good side, all pulling together and complementing each other well. Lara aside, they are best described as workmanlike, rather than blessed with lashings of natural talent, but any side on this sort of winning run is going to be extremely hard to beat.

A pleasurable duty today was along with Dermot Reeve to present awards to young cricketers who are part of Ian Waring's youth development scheme. After this process we surprised Ed Giddins by awarding him his county cap. The announcement over the tannoy was the first Giddo had heard of it and I was delighted to reward him for all his hard work and application this season. The process is for the captain to make a recommendation to the committee, who then consider and approve the award. It's a proud moment in any cricketer's career and a few glasses of champagne were consumed in the bar after the game.

To be able to take the field wearing the six Martlets means everything to a Sussex player, and it reminded me of when I was capped in 1986 at Hove. It's always a surprise and for me it happened during the tea interval when I was batting against Notts. I had been striving for my cap for a few years, and when I walked on the field after tea to continue my innings the first person to congratulate me was Richard Hadlee. It's a special moment you never forget. You really feel that you have arrived as a professional cricketer. As captain it is a pleasure to present such an honour to emerging players, and to share their joy.

30 August - Essex at Chelmsford, first day
The game with Essex has been brought forward as the Nat West final takes place on Saturday. This time last year we were looking forward to the final at Lords. I remember the press intimating that an interesting sub-plot was Dermot Reeve, the ex-Sussex player, versus Alan Wells, the Sussex captain searching for one last score to force his way into the England side to tour the West Indies. I remember walking out to bat at Lords thinking of nothing other than playing my natural game and helping Sussex win the trophy. As far as touring was concerned, I assumed the selectors had made up their minds by then on who was going where. After a good season last year I was waiting on tenterhooks right to the end. This year I've had a dreadful season with the bat yet I already know that I'll be captain of the A tour to India. Such is life.

Essex are always hard to beat, especially so at Chelmsford, and they are well placed in the pack closing in behind Warwickshire for the prize money positions in the championship table. Both sides wanted to bat, on a used wicket destined to wear, and the toss was the only thing we won all day. We lost wickets with the alarming regularity I have come to dread this season, and only a dashing 73 from Speighty, and some spirited late resistance from Sals saved us from being dismissed for another embarrassingly low total. The 246 we made was never going to be enough on a 350 wicket and Essex breezed along to 34 without loss in less than seven overs.

It was a strange day with some indifferent bowling and resultant high scoring overs, interspersed with the clatter of self-destruction. Jamie Hall's was the only genuine dismissal. Everyone else didn't require any help from the bowlers to get out as we all played horrendous strokes to get ourselves out. I can only put it down to a lack of confidence on the batting side, yet we should be feeding off the tremendous performances the bowlers have put in.

I fell to a real sucker punch from Mark Ilott. He bowled me a short ball which I shaped to pull, but it hardly bounced. I immediately thought that if he tries to bounce me again it will be faster, and instead of going after it with the hook I'll let it fly past. He pitched it short again and in the course of letting it go the ball struck my gloves and lobbed up to the keeper. If I was in a confident state of mind I would have pulled the ball to the boundary without hesitation. When you're scoring runs your mind is clear and you enter another zone. When runs are hard to come by your mind is racing away looking for ways to break out of a bad patch, and not surprisingly the art of batting becomes infinitely more difficult.

This is the first good batting wicket we've played on for eight weeks, and I can't believe we didn't capitalise. In part, it's down to having batted recently on indifferent wickets and having become used to trying to survive rather than build an innings.

31 August - Essex, second day

For the first time this season the bowlers were unable to come to the rescue and repair the damage of a batting failure. The recently capped Nick Night scored 157, Gooch 79 and Irani 67. We will have to bowl well to keep the score under 400, and even then our batting will need to be transformed to set any sort of hard-to-get target for Essex's last innings. The prospects of a win are receding with every run they score, but we must do all we can to deny them the winning points. It was uncharacteristic of us to give such a lethargic performance in the field. At lunch Giffy felt it necessary to remind the team that we are only 10 points behind second place, and there is both prize money and pride at stake, and not necessarily in that order.

The end of one season means it's time to prepare for the next, and Giffy and myself had a meeting over dinner with the officers of the club to put forward our views on our playing requirements for next year. The club has to move on and it's an important part of the captain's duties to discuss the playing needs for the future.

1 September- Essex, third day

We achieved our first objective which was to restrict them to a score in the region of 400. Giddo again bowled with discipline and patience, returning figures of five for 83, a spirited achievement on a batting wicket. Within a few overs Mark Ilott struck twice and we were four for two, Billy Athey and Neil Lenham back in the pavilion for nought. Jamie Hall and myself saw us through to lunch, then play was frequently interrupted by rain and bad light. It is always difficult to maintain your concentration under those circumstances, and it didn't make our task any easier. Mark Ilott got me out for the second time in the match, padding up to a ball swinging in to me. Speighty was unlucky to fall just short of his fifty. We struggled along to 187 for six and saving the game tomorrow will be a hard task. We will have to bat for a long time, on a wicket which is starting to break up and being exploited by Peter Such.

2 September - Essex, final day
We fought well this morning. Had we shown such fight and determination in the first innings then it could have been a completely different game. The total of 277 we ended up with was above par on a wicket which became a turning dust-bowl. The most unlikely, yet the most gutsy, effort of the day was a partnership of 51 between Sals and Giddo for the last wicket. We all know that Sals can bat but Giddo is less known for his occupation of the crease. He scored a career-best 24 in flamboyant style, providing rich entertainment for his team-mates by hitting Peter Such for three straight sixes. It cheered us up no end at a time when we realised the game was slipping away.

There was a brief ray of hope when Gooch was out in Sals' first over, and he then took two quick wickets to reduce them to 37 for three. Any hopes of having them on the rack were dispelled by Nick Knight and Ronnie Irani as they knocked off the runs needed for victory, to win the game by seven wickets.

Again we lost because we failed to perform as a batting unit, and the dressing room is dominated by talk of how the batsmen are letting down the bowlers. We need to sit down and pump some confidence into the batsman for our last game, as a good performance then will contribute towards putting this year's batting disasters behind us. In my time at Sussex there has never been a greater contrast between the two major components of our play. When we're bowling, the expectancy of success is always there, and not once this year have I been reduced to wondering where the next wicket will come from. When we're batting, the fear of failure means that we expect to get out rather than score runs. This is why a more positive approach is needed, as for a batsman to limit his expectations to survival is self-defeating.

The winter touring parties were announced today and I paid close attention to the players selected to accompany me to India. To see Darren Gough, John Crawley, Steve Rhodes and Martin McCague in the side for Australia gives me a thrill after touring with them in South Africa. I know how proud Gough is to be representing his country and he will try his heart out for England. I remember saying to John Crawley that I would not be surprised to see him playing Test cricket this summer. I was surprised that they chose as many as 16 players for my tour, but we need sufficient to cover for the fitness problems which materialise in India. It's a well-chosen and balanced side, with four spinners, all-rounders, and promising young batsmen. Having just witnessed Nick Knight's promise with the bat I can vouch for his selection. For an opening batsman to play spin as well as he does is a rarity. I am looking forward to being briefed by the selectors as to their expectations for the tour, so I can plan my tactics accordingly. I am particularly delighted that John Barclay has been appointed tour manager as I know him well. Sals is also in the party, and if the tour was anywhere but India I genuinely feel that Giddo would have been a strong contender for a place in the squad. He knew that he was knocking on the door and I detected a sense of disappointment that he wasn't selected.

There's a break at the end of the season to recharge the batteries then training sessions at Lilleshall and a pre-tour trip to Malaga. I've also asked the Sussex physio for a training programme to fully prepare me for the tour. At the end of a season it's as important to rest the mind as well as the body, especially as captain, because during the season your mind is tuned to nothing but cricket. A short period of reflection, followed by an opportunity to relax and to think about something else, is a mental tonic essential to maintain the right mix of clarity of purpose, dedication and enthusiasm.

4 September - Essex, Sunday League
I've said this far too often this season, but yet again we

played abominably and lost a one-day game. I played Nicky Phillips instead of Sals because I didn't expect the ball to spin too much and preferred the control of a finger spinner rather than a wrist spinner. It's also an opportunity to blood young players and give them some experience. The seamers got us off to a good start but John Stephenson and Nasser Hussain shared a partnership of over 100 and they managed a total of 207.

Peter Moores suggested that instead of sending in a big hitter at three, Franklyn should open the batting with Billy Athey. We lost Franklyn and Keith Greenfield early on, but with batting to come I expected to mount a serious challenge to the Essex total. I wasn't timing the ball at all and in 25 runs never hit a boundary. This built up the pressure on Speighty at the other end so I decided to hit out, but only succeeded in chipping a catch to extra cover. Speighty eventually fell having to try and win the game on his own, because wickets were falling at the other end.

I need to consider some different tactics for next year and will think along the lines of sticking with what I consider to be the right batting order for our one-day cricket, rather than chopping and changing in response to specific results. Given that we have lacked consistency in the Sunday League, I must at least be consistent with the batting order so that the team has a chance to settle and understand the tactics.

15 September - *Yorkshire at Hove, first day*
Due to rain, only six overs were possible today. I won

the toss and decided to bat on a white wicket from which we shaved off all the grass evident when we played Warwickshire in the last game at Hove. With our batsmen lacking form and confidence I felt a wicket less suited to a seam attack would give us a better chance of winning the game, weather permitting.

At the start of the day I spoke to all the players, recognising that a certain amount of end of season joviality was in the air. I stressed that although this is the last game of the season, I see it as the start of what I want Sussex to achieve next year, and that is to build upon the good things we have done this year in terms of taking wickets, playing pressure cricket and winning championship games. It was nice to hear from some of the guys that far from feeling jaded they wish the season was just starting.

16 September - Yorkshire, second day

Another indifferent batting display after Billy Athey and Neil Lenham had worked hard to see off the new ball, in the face of some good bowling from Yorkshire. We slumped to 62 for four before myself and Moorsey staged a partial recovery. The ball was seaming around, and for what seemed to be the first time this season I rode my luck to go on and make a decent score - 84. I had a good net session in the middle before play and never felt less than positive when batting. Unfortunately, I never found a batsman at the other end to build a substantial partnership with and we were all out for an inadequate 226. Other than a good opening spell from Franklyn, the Yorkshire batsmen set about some weak bowling and raced away to close at 109 for two.

17 September - Yorkshire, third day

I started the day fearing that if Yorkshire batted on to a decent lead we would be out of the game completely. The bowlers atoned for their indifferent display yesterday and restricted Yorkshire to a negligible lead of 20. In the morning session we placed a stranglehold on the batsmen from which they were never able to break free. Giddo did particularly well and took four wickets. The ball is still seaming around off a moist wicket and only batsmen with a positive approach have scored runs. It is not a wicket for batting out time, as sooner or later a ball does something and you're out.

The positive approach I was looking for failed to register with the players, except myself and Moorsey who scored 55 each and helped the side to reach 181 for eight in 50 overs. We need to be defending at least 180-200 in the last innings, so it is imperative to eke out a few more runs in the morning. One thing that has struck me in this game is that half of our dismissals have been lbw, a high percentage on a seaming wicket.

18 September - Yorkshire, Sunday League

Another Sunday, another lousy performance, and another loss. Having said that, we did decide to play a few youngsters to give them some experience: Keith Newell who has had a particularly good season in the second-team, scoring nearly 2000 runs in all competitions; Toby Pierce, a left-handed batsman down from Durham University; Nicky Phillips, who has played a few Sunday games this season. David Byas got Yorkshire off to a solid start, and Ashley Metcalfe, coming in at six, was particularly aggressive towards the end. After recovering slightly we conceded 54 telling runs in the last four overs. Carlos did well and I am pleased with the progress he's made with his bowling this season. Next year he must look to make the same strides forward with his batting.

A total of 214 was within our reach but we got off to a dreadful start, losing three wickets for little more than 20 runs. Keith Greenfield and myself shared a good partnership of almost 100 before he hit the spinner down long off's throat. Keith has a tendency to get himself out in one-day games after all the hard work of getting set. I wasn't happy to see him self-destruct in this fashion, and I'll be discussing with him how it's time for him to improve his one-day performances by going on to make the match-winning scores I know he is capable of. We were chasing nearly 10 an over towards the end, and with Darren Gough bowling yorker after yorker we fell short. He attacked the stumps expertly, making run scoring very difficult, and picking up his best Sunday League figures with five for 13.

19 September - Yorkshire, final day
A wet, miserable, and anti-climactic end to the season with no play possible at all. The rain washed away our remaining hopes of finishing in the top five in the championship. It gave what should be a jolly day a

somewhat melancholy flavour, with players dispersing and going their separate ways for the winter.

This year has been no different to the last two in that I continue to learn about captaincy and to build winning relationships with the team. It has been a good season as far as our learning is concerned, and I recognise that it takes time to build a championship winning side. Giffy and myself will get together several times over the winter to formulate our plans for next year. I firmly believe that we have the makings of a championship-winning side at Sussex and I know that every player on the staff will be spending this winter in preparation for a dedicated assault next year.

This is the end of my 14th season and I cannot believe how fast the time has passed this year. No matter how good or how poor the season has been from a personal point of view, I look back each year and realise that it is a great privilege to be playing professional cricket for Sussex, especially with the additional honour of being captain. There is nothing else I'd rather be doing.